Jupyter for Data Science

Exploratory analysis, statistical modeling, machine learning,
and data visualization with Jupyter

Dan Toomey

BIRMINGHAM - MUMBAI

Jupyter for Data Science

First published: October 2017

Production reference: 1171017

Published by Packt Publishing Ltd.
Livery Place
35 Livery Street
Birmingham
B3 2PB, UK.

ISBN 978-1-78588-007-0

www.packtpub.com

Credits

Author
Dan Toomey

Reviewers
Jesse Bacon
Ruben Oliva Ramos

Commissioning Editor
Amey Varangaonkar

Acquisition Editor
Amey Varangaonkar

Content Development Editor
Aishwarya Pandere

Technical Editor
Prasad Ramesh

Copy Editor
Safis Editing

Project Coordinator
Nidhi Joshi

Proofreader
Safis Editing

Indexer
Tejal Daruwale Soni

Graphics
Tania Dutta

Production Coordinator
Aparna Bhagat

About the Author

Dan Toomey has been developing applications for over 20 years. He has worked in a variety of industries and companies of all sizes, in roles from sole contributor to VP/CTO level. For the last 10 years or so, he has been contracting companies in the eastern Massachusetts area under Dan Toomey Software Corp. Dan has also written *R for Data Science* and *Learning Jupyter* with Packt Publishing.

About the Reviewers

Jesse Bacon is a hobbyist programmer and technologist in the Washington D.C. metro area. In his free time, he mostly studies a new and interesting technology or visits the gym pursuing fitness goals. Jesse values the opinions of the development community and looks forward to a new generation of programmers with all the gifts of today's computing environments.

Ruben Oliva Ramos is a computer systems engineer from Tecnologico of León Institute, with a master's degree in computer and electronic systems engineering, teleinformatics, and networking specialization from the University of Salle Bajio in Leon, Guanajuato Mexico. He has more than 5 years of experience in developing web applications to control and monitor devices connected with Arduino and Raspberry Pi using web frameworks and cloud services to build Internet of Things applications.

He is a mechatronics teacher at the University of Salle Bajio and teaches students of master's in design and engineering of mechatronics systems. He also works at Centro de Bachillerato Tecnologico Industrial 225 in Leon, teaching electronics, robotics and control, automation, and microcontrollers at Mechatronics Technician Career.

Ruben is a consultant and developer projects in areas such as monitoring systems and datalogger data using technologies such as Android, iOS, Windows Phone, HTML5, PHP, CSS, Ajax, JavaScript, Angular, ASP .NET databases (SQlite, mongoDB, and MySQL), web servers (Node.js and IIS), hardware programming (Arduino, Raspberry pi, Ethernet Shield, GPS and GSM/GPRS, ESP8266), and control and monitor systems for data acquisition and programming.

He is the author of these two books for Packt Publishing:

- Internet of Things Programming with JavaScript
- Advanced Analytics with R and Tableau

Also Monitoring, controlling and acquisition of data with Arduino and Visual Basic .NET for Alfaomega.

I would like to thank my savior and lord, Jesus Christ, for giving me the strength and courage to pursue this project; to my dearest wife, Mayte; our two lovely sons, Ruben and Dario; my dear father, Ruben; my dearest mom Rosalia; my brother, Juan Tomas; and my sister, Rosalia, whom I love. This is for all their support while reviewing this book, for allowing me to pursue my dream and tolerating not being with them after my busy day. I'm very grateful to Packt Publishing for giving the opportunity to collaborate as an author and reviewer and join to this honest and professional team.

www.PacktPub.com

For support files and downloads related to your book, please visit www.PacktPub.com. Did you know that Packt offers eBook versions of every book published, with PDF and ePub files available? You can upgrade to the eBook version at www.PacktPub.com and as a print book customer, you are entitled to a discount on the eBook copy. Get in touch with us at service@packtpub.com for more details. At www.PacktPub.com, you can also read a collection of free technical articles, sign up for a range of free newsletters and receive exclusive discounts and offers on Packt books and eBooks.

https://www.packtpub.com/mapt

Get the most in-demand software skills with Mapt. Mapt gives you full access to all Packt books and video courses, as well as industry-leading tools to help you plan your personal development and advance your career.

Why subscribe?

- Fully searchable across every book published by Packt
- Copy and paste, print, and bookmark content
- On demand and accessible via a web browser

Customer Feedback

Thanks for purchasing this Packt book. At Packt, quality is at the heart of our editorial process. To help us improve, please leave us an honest review on this book's Amazon page at https://www.amazon.com/dp/1785880071.

If you'd like to join our team of regular reviewers, you can email us at customerreviews@packtpub.com. We award our regular reviewers with free eBooks and videos in exchange for their valuable feedback. Help us be relentless in improving our products!

Table of Contents

Preface   1

Chapter 1: Jupyter and Data Science   7

  Jupyter concepts   7
  A first look at the Jupyter user interface   8
    Detailing the Jupyter tabs   8
    What actions can I perform with Jupyter?   9
    What objects can Jupyter manipulate?   11
    Viewing the Jupyter project display   12
      File menu   13
      Edit menu   14
      View menu   15
      Insert menu   16
      Cell menu   16
      Kernel menu   17
      Help menu   18
      Icon toolbar   18
    How does it look when we execute scripts?   19
    Industry data science usage   20
    Real life examples   21
      Finance, Python - European call option valuation   21
      Finance, Python - Monte Carlo pricing   23
      Gambling, R - betting analysis   25
      Insurance, R - non-life insurance pricing 27
      Consumer products, R - marketing effectiveness   31
    Using Docker with Jupyter   34
      Using a public Docker service   35
      Installing Docker on your machine   36
    How to share notebooks with others   36
      Can you email a notebook?   36
      Sharing a notebook on Google Drive   37
      Sharing on GitHub   37
      Store as HTML on a web server   37
      Install Jupyter on a web server   37
    How can you secure a notebook?   38
      Access control   38
      Malicious content   38
  Summary   39

Chapter 2: Working with Analytical Data on Jupyter   41

Data scraping with a Python notebook	41
Using heavy-duty data processing functions in Jupyter	45
Using NumPy functions in Jupyter	45
Using pandas in Jupyter	48
Use pandas to read text files in Jupyter	48
Use pandas to read Excel files in Jupyter	49
Using pandas to work with data frames	50
Using the groupby function in a data frame	50
Manipulating columns in a data frame	51
Calculating outliers in a data frame	52
Using SciPy in Jupyter	53
Using SciPy integration in Jupyter	53
Using SciPy optimization in Jupyter	55
Using SciPy interpolation in Jupyter	56
Using SciPy Fourier Transforms in Jupyter	58
Using SciPy linear algebra in Jupyter	59
Expanding on panda data frames in Jupyter	61
Sorting and filtering data frames in Jupyter/IPython	63
Filtering a data frame	63
Sorting a data frame	64
Summary	66
Chapter 3: Data Visualization and Prediction	67
Make a prediction using scikit-learn	67
Make a prediction using R	72
Interactive visualization	77
Plotting using Plotly	79
Creating a human density map	80
Draw a histogram of social data	83
Plotting 3D data	86
Summary	88
Chapter 4: Data Mining and SQL Queries	89
Special note for Windows installation	90
Using Spark to analyze data	90
Another MapReduce example	92
Using SparkSession and SQL	94
Combining datasets	97
Loading JSON into Spark	101
Using Spark pivot	103
Summary	105

Chapter 5: R with Jupyter   107
How to set up R for Jupyter   107
R data analysis of the 2016 US election demographics   108
Analyzing 2016 voter registration and voting   111
Analyzing changes in college admissions   120
Predicting airplane arrival time   126
Summary   130

Chapter 6: Data Wrangling   131
Reading a CSV file   131
Reading another CSV file   135
Manipulating data with dplyr   138
    Converting a data frame to a dplyr table   139
    Getting a quick overview of the data value ranges   139
Sampling a dataset   140
    Filtering rows in a data frame   142
    Adding a column to a data frame   143
    Obtaining a summary on a calculated field   144
    Piping data between functions   144
    Obtaining the 99% quantile   145
    Obtaining a summary on grouped data   146
Tidying up data with tidyr   147
Summary   152

Chapter 7: Jupyter Dashboards   153
Visualizing glyph ready data   153
Publishing a notebook   159
    Font markdown   159
    List markdown   160
    Heading markdown   160
    Table markdown   161
    Code markdown   161
    More markdown   162
Creating a Shiny dashboard   162
    R application coding   163
    Publishing your dashboard   167
Building standalone dashboards   168
Summary   170

Chapter 8: Statistical Modeling   171

Converting JSON to CSV   171
Evaluating Yelp reviews   172
   Summary data   173
   Review spread   174
   Finding the top rated firms   175
   Finding the most rated firms   176
   Finding all ratings for a top rated firm   176
   Determining the correlation between ratings and number of reviews   178
   Building a model of reviews   179
Using Python to compare ratings   180
Visualizing average ratings by cuisine   182
Arbitrary search of ratings   183
Determining relationships between number of ratings and ratings   184
   Summary   188

Chapter 9: Machine Learning Using Jupyter   189
  Naive Bayes   189
   Naive Bayes using R   189
   Naive Bayes using Python   192
  Nearest neighbor estimator   193
   Nearest neighbor using R   193
   Nearest neighbor using Python   195
  Decision trees   198
   Decision trees in R   199
   Decision trees in Python   201
  Neural networks   203
   Neural networks in R   203
  Random forests   205
   Random forests in R   206
  Summary   207

Chapter 10: Optimizing Jupyter Notebooks   209
  Deploying notebooks   209
   Deploying to JupyterHub   209
    Installing JupyterHub   210
    Accessing a JupyterHub Installation   210
   Jupyter hosting   211
  Optimizing your script   212
   Optimizing your Python scripts   212
    Determining how long a script takes   212
    Using Python regular expressions   213

Using Python string handling	213
Minimizing loop operations	213
Profiling your script	214
Optimizing your R scripts	214
Using microbenchmark to profile R script	214
Modifying provided functionality	215
Optimizing name lookup	215
Optimizing data frame value extraction	215
Changing R Implementation	216
Changing algorithms	216
Monitoring Jupyter	216
Caching your notebook	217
Securing a notebook	217
Managing notebook authorization	217
Securing notebook content	217
Scaling Jupyter Notebooks	218
Sharing Jupyter Notebooks	218
Sharing Jupyter Notebook on a notebook server	218
Sharing encrypted Jupyter Notebook on a notebook server	219
Sharing notebook on a web server	219
Sharing notebook on Docker	219
Converting a notebook	220
Versioning a notebook	220
Summary	221
Index	223

Preface

Jupyter is an open platform that is growing in use. Jupyter can have programs written in a variety of languages. Many of these languages are geared towards data science, such as R and Python. In this book, we'll look at solving data science problems using a variety of languages on the Jupyter platform.

We will start by looking into some of the basics of Jupyter. Then we will use Jupyter as the platform for our data analysis and visualizations. We'll look into data mining, data wrangling, and machine learning, all under the auspices of the Jupyter framework.

You will learn how to use Jupyter to solve your data science problems using a suite of programming languages.

What this book covers

Chapter 1, *Jupyter and Data Science*, covers the details of the Jupyter user interface: what objects it works with and what actions can be taken by Jupyter. We'll see what the display tells us about the data, what tools are available, and some real-life examples from the industry showing R and Python coding. We will also see some of the ways to share our notebook with other users and, correspondingly, how to protect our notebook with different security mechanisms.

Chapter 2, *Working with Analytical Data in Jupyter*, covers using Python to scrape a website to gather data for analysis. Then we use Python NumPy, pandas, and SciPy functions for in-depth computations of results. The chapter goes further into pandas and explores manipulating data frames. Lastly, it shows examples of sorting and filtering data frames.

Chapter 3, *Data Visualization and Prediction*, demonstrates prediction models from Python and R under Jupyter. Then it uses Matplotlib for data visualization and interactive plotting (under Python). Then it covers several graphing techniques available in Jupyter and density maps with SciPy. We use histograms to visualize social data. Lastly, we generate a 3D plot in Jupyter.

Chapter 4, *Data Mining and SQL Queries*, covers Spark Context. We show examples of using Hadoop map/reduce and use SQL with Spark data. Then we combine data frames, operate on the resulting set, import JSON data, and manipulate it with Spark. Lastly, we look at using a pivot to gather information about a data frame.

Chapter 5, *R on Jupyter*, covers setting up R to be one of the engines available for a notebook. Then we use some rudimentary R to analyze voter demographics for a presidential election and trends in college admissions. Finally, we look at using a predictive model to determine whether some flights would be delayed or not.

Chapter 6, *Data Wrangling*, teaches reading in CSV files and performing some quick analysis of the data, including visualizations to help understand the data. Next, we consider some of the functions available in the dplyr package. We also use piping to more easily transfer the results of one operation into another operation. Lastly, we look into using the tidyr package to clean up or tidy up our data.

Chapter 7, *Jupyter Dashboards*, covers visualizing data graphically using glyphs to emphasize important aspects of the data. We use markdown to annotate a notebook page and Shiny to generate an interactive application. We show a way to host notebooks outside of Jupyter.

Chapter 8, *Statistical Modeling*, teaches converting a JSON file to a CSV file. We evaluate the yelp cuisine review dataset, determining the top rated and most rated firms. We use Python to perform a similar evaluation of yelp business ratings, finding very similar distributions of the data.

Chapter 9, *Machine Learning Using Jupyter*, covers several machine learning algorithms in both R and Python to compare and contrast. We use naive Bayes to determine how the data might be used. We apply nearest neighbor in a couple of different ways to see results. We also use decision trees to come up with an algorithm for predictions and a neural net to explain housing prices. Finally, we use a random forest algorithm to do the same.

Chapter 10, *Optimizing Jupyter Notebooks*, deploys your notebook so that others can access it. It shows optimizations you can make to increase your notebook's performance. Then we look at securing the notebook and the mechanisms of sharing it.

What you need for this book

This book is focused on using Jupyter as the platform for data science. It assumes that you have a good understanding of the data science concepts and are looking to use Jupyter as your presentation platform.

Who this book is for

This book is for data science practitioners who are looking to publicize their findings while still retaining the essence of their research. With Jupyter, you can portray your exact methodology in a interactive manner.

Conventions

In this book, you will find a number of text styles that distinguish between different kinds of information. Here are some examples of these styles and an explanation of their meaning. Code words in text, database table names, folder names, filenames, file extensions, pathnames, dummy URLs, user input, and Twitter handles are shown as follows: "Similarly, the preceding `describe` statement gives us some quick statistics on the data frame."

A block of code is set as follows:

```
plt.xlabel("Actual Price")
plt.ylabel("Predicted Price")
plt.title("Actual Price vs Predicted Price")
```

New terms and **important words** are shown in bold.

Words that you see on the screen, for example, in menus or dialog boxes, appear in the text like this: "The **Running** tab lists the notebooks that have been started."

 Warnings or important notes appear like this.

 Tips and tricks appear like this.

Reader feedback

Feedback from our readers is always welcome. Let us know what you think about this book-what you liked or disliked. Reader feedback is important for us as it helps us develop titles that you will really get the most out of. To send us general feedback, simply email feedback@packtpub.com, and mention the book's title in the subject of your message. If there is a topic that you have expertise in and you are interested in either writing or contributing to a book, see our author guide at www.packtpub.com/authors.

Customer support

Now that you are the proud owner of a Packt book, we have a number of things to help you to get the most from your purchase.

Downloading the example code

You can download the example code files for this book from your account at http://www.packtpub.com. If you purchased this book elsewhere, you can visit http://www.packtpub.com/support and register to have the files emailed directly to you. You can download the code files by following these steps:

1. Log in or register to our website using your email address and password.
2. Hover the mouse pointer on the **SUPPORT** tab at the top.
3. Click on **Code Downloads & Errata**.
4. Enter the name of the book in the **Search** box.
5. Select the book for which you're looking to download the code files.
6. Choose from the drop-down menu where you purchased this book from.
7. Click on **Code Download**.

Once the file is downloaded, please make sure that you unzip or extract the folder using the latest version of:

- WinRAR / 7-Zip for Windows
- Zipeg / iZip / UnRarX for Mac
- 7-Zip / PeaZip for Linux

The code bundle for the book is also hosted on GitHub at `https://github.com/PacktPublishing/Jupyter-for-Data-Science`. We also have other code bundles from our rich catalog of books and videos available at `https://github.com/PacktPublishing/`. Check them out!

Errata

Although we have taken every care to ensure the accuracy of our content, mistakes do happen. If you find a mistake in one of our books-maybe a mistake in the text or the code-we would be grateful if you could report this to us. By doing so, you can save other readers from frustration and help us improve subsequent versions of this book. If you find any errata, please report them by visiting `http://www.packtpub.com/submit-errata`, selecting your book, clicking on the **Errata Submission Form** link, and entering the details of your errata. Once your errata are verified, your submission will be accepted and the errata will be uploaded to our website or added to any list of existing errata under the Errata section of that title. To view the previously submitted errata, go to `https://www.packtpub.com/books/content/support` and enter the name of the book in the search field. The required information will appear under the **Errata** section.

Piracy

Piracy of copyrighted material on the internet is an ongoing problem across all media. At Packt, we take the protection of our copyright and licenses very seriously. If you come across any illegal copies of our works in any form on the internet, please provide us with the location address or website name immediately so that we can pursue a remedy. Please contact us at `copyright@packtpub.com` with a link to the suspected pirated material. We appreciate your help in protecting our authors and our ability to bring you valuable content.

Questions

If you have a problem with any aspect of this book, you can contact us at `questions@packtpub.com`, and we will do our best to address the problem.

1
Jupyter and Data Science

The Jupyter product was derived from the IPython project. The IPython project was used to provide interactive online access to Python. Over time it became useful to interact with other programming languages, such as R, in the same manner. With this split from only Python, the tool grew into its current manifestation of Jupyter. IPython is still an active tool available for use.

Jupyter is available as a web application for a wide variety of platforms. It can also be used on your desktop/laptop over a wide variety of installations. In this book, we will be exploring using Jupyter from a Windows PC and over the internet for other providers.

Jupyter concepts

Jupyter is organized around a few basic concepts:

- **Notebook**: A collection of statements (in a language). For example, this could be a complete R script that loads data, analyzes it, produces a graph, and records results elsewhere.
- **Cell**: the lowest granular piece of a Jupyter Notebook that can be worked with:
    - **Current Cell**: The current cell being edited or the one(s) selected
- **Kernel**: each notebook is associated with a specific language implementation. The part of Jupyter which processes the specific language involved is called a kernel.

A first look at the Jupyter user interface

We can jump right in and see what Jupyter has to offer. A Jupyter screen looks like this:

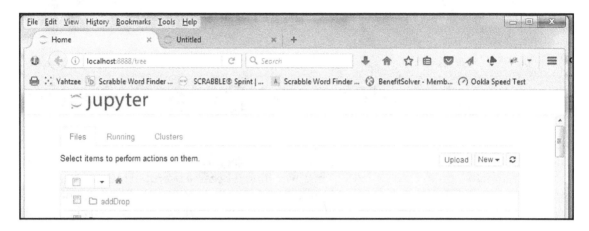

So, Jupyter is deployed as a website that can be accessed on your machine (or can be accessed like any other website across the internet).

We see the URL of the page, `http://localhost:8888/tree`. `localhost` is a pseudonym for a web server running on your machine. The website we are accessing on the web server is in a *tree* display. This is the default display. This conforms to the display of the projects within Jupyter. Jupyter displays objects in a tree layout much like Windows File Explorer. The main page lists a number of projects; each project is its own subdirectory and contains a further delineation of content for each. Depending on where you start Jupyter, the existing contents of the current directory will be included in the display as well.

Detailing the Jupyter tabs

On the web page, we have the soon to be familiar Jupyter logo and three tabs:

- **Files**
- **Running**
- **Clusters**

The **Files** tab lists the objects available to Jupyter. The files used by Jupyter are stored as regular files on your disk. Jupyter provides context managers that know how to process the different types of files and programs you are using. You can see the Jupyter files when you use Windows Explorer to view your file contents (they have an `.ipynb` file extension). You can see non-Jupyter files listed in the Jupyter window as well.

The **Running** tab lists the notebooks that have been started. Jupyter keeps track of which notebooks are running. This tab allows you to control which notebooks are running at any time.

The **Clusters** tab is for environments where several machines are in use for running Jupyter.

 Cluster implementations of Jupyter are a topic worthy of their own, dedicated materials.

What actions can I perform with Jupyter?

Next, we see:

- A prompt **Select items to perform action**
- An **Upload** button
- A **New** pull down menu and
- A Refresh icon

The prompt tells you that you can select multiple items and then perform the same action on all of them. Most of the following actions (in the menus) can be performed over a single item or a selected set of items.

The **Upload** button will present a prompt to select a file to upload to Jupyter. This would typically be used to move a data file into the project for access in the case where Jupyter is running as a website in a remote location where you can't just copy the file to the disk where Jupyter is running.

The **New** pull down menu presents a list of choices of the different kinds of Jupyter projects (kernels) that are available:

We can see the list of objects that Jupyter knows how to create:

- **Text File**: Create a text file for use in this folder. For example, if the notebook were to import a file you may create the file using this feature.
- **Folder**: Yes, just like in Windows File Explorer.
- **Terminals Unavailable**: Grayed out, this feature can be used in a Nix environment.
- **Notebooks**: Grayed out,-this is not really a file type, but a heading to the different types of notebooks that this installation knows how to create.
- **Julia 0.4.5**: Creates a Julia notebook where the coding is in the Julia language.
- **Python 3**: Creates a notebook where the coding is in the Python language. This is the default.
- **R**: Creates a notebook where the coding is in the R language.
- Depending on which kernels you have installed in your installation, you may see other notebook types listed.

What objects can Jupyter manipulate?

If we started one of the notebooks (it would automatically be selected in the Jupyter object list) and now looked at the pulldown of actions against the objects selected we would see a display like the following:

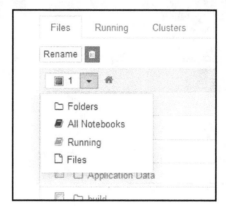

We see that the menu action has changed to **Rename**, as that is the most likely action to be taken on one file and we have an icon to delete the project as well (the trashcan icon).

The item count is now **1** (we have one object selected in the list), the icon for the one item is a filled in blue square (denoting that it is a running project), and a familiar Home icon to bring us back to the Jupyter home page display in the previous screenshot.

The object's menu has choices for:

- **Folders**: select the folders available
- **All Notebooks**: select the Jupyter Notebooks
- **Running**: select the running Jupyter Notebooks
- **Files**: select the files in the directory

If we scroll down in the object display, we see a little different information in the list of objects available. Each of the objects listed has a type (denoted by the icon shape associated) and a name assigned by the user when it was created.

Each of the objects is a Jupyter project that can be accessed, shared, and moved on its own. Every project has a full name, as entered by the user creating the project, and an icon that portrays this entry as a project. We will see other Jupyter icons corresponding to other project components, as follows:

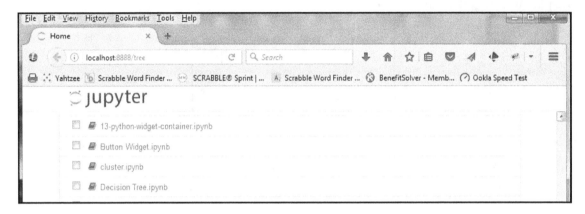

Viewing the Jupyter project display

If we pull down the **New** menu and select **Python 3**, Jupyter would create a new Python notebook and move to display its contents. We would see a display like the following:

We have created a new Jupyter Notebook and are in its display. The logo is there. The title defaults to Untitled, which we can change by clicking on it. There is an **(autosaved)** marker that tells you Jupyter has automatically stored your notebook to disk (and will continue to do so regularly as you work on it).

We now have a menu bar and a denotation that this notebook is using Python 3 as its source language. The menu choices are:

- **File**: Standard file operations
- **Edit**: For editing cell contents (more to come)
- **View**: To change the display of the notebook
- **Insert**: To insert a cell in the notebook
- **Cell**: To change the format, usage of a cell
- **Kernel**: To adjust the kernel used for the notebook
- **Help:** To bring up the help system for Jupyter

File menu

The **File** menu has the following choices:

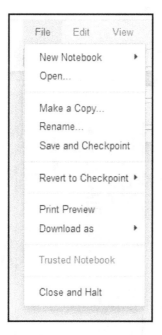

- **New Notebook**: Similar to the pull down from the home page.
- **Open...**: Open a notebook.
- **Make a Copy...**: Copy a notebook.
- **Rename...**: Rename a notebook.

- **Save and Checkpoint**: Save the current notebook at a checkpoint. Checkpoints are specific points in a notebook's history that you want to maintain in order to return to a checkpoint if you change your mind about a recent set of changes.
- **Print Preview**: Similar to any print preview that you have used otherwise.
- **Download as**: Allows you to store the notebook in a variety of formats. The most notable formats would be PDF or Excel, which would allow you to share the notebook with users that do not have access to Jupyter.
- **Trusted Notebook**: (The feature is grayed out). When a notebook is opened by a user, the server computes a signature with the user's key, and compares it with the signature stored in the notebook's metadata. If the signature matches, HTML and JavaScript output in the notebook will be trusted at load, otherwise it will be untrusted.
- **Close and Halt**: Close the current notebook and stop it running in the Jupyter system.

Edit menu

The **Edit** menu has the following choices:

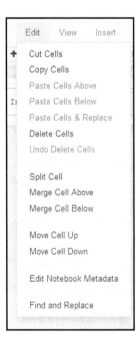

- **Cut Cells**: Typical cut operation.
- **Copy Cells**: Assuming you are used to the GUI operations of copying cells to memory buffer and later pasting into another location in the notebook.
- **Paste Cells Above**: If you have selected a cell and if you have copied a cell, this option will not be grayed out and will paste the buffered cell above the current cell.
- **Paste Cells Below**: Similar to the previous option.
- **Delete Cells**: Will delete the selected cells.
- **Undo Delete Cells**.
- **Split Cell**: There is a style issue here, regarding how many statements you put into a cell. Many times, you will start with one cell containing a number of statements and split that cell up many times to break off individual or groups of statements into their own cell.
- **Merge Cell Above**: Combine the current cell with the one above it.
- **Merge Cell Below**: Similar to the previous option.
- **Move Cell Up**: Move the current cell before the one above it.
- **Move Cell Down**.
- **Edit Notebook Metadata**: For advanced users to modify the internal programming language used by Jupyter for your notebook.
- **Find and Replace**: Locate specific text within cells and possibly replace.

View menu

The **View** menu has the following choices:

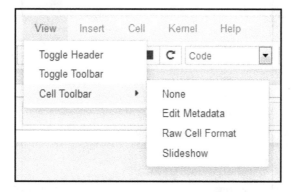

- **Toggle Header**: Toggle the display of the Jupyter header
- **Toggle Toolbar**: Toggle the display of the Jupyter toolbar

- **Cell Toolbar**: Change the displayed items for the cell being edited:
  - **None**: Don't display a cell toolbar
  - **Edit Metadata**: Edit a cells metadata directly
  - **Raw Cell Format**: Edit the cell raw format as used by Jupyter
  - **Slideshow**: Walk through the cells in a slideshow manner

Insert menu

The **Insert** menu has the following choices:

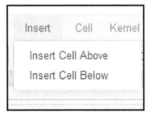

- **Insert Cell Above**: Insert the copied buffer cell in front of the current cell
- **Insert Cell Below**: Same as previous one

Cell menu

The **Cell** menu has the following choices:

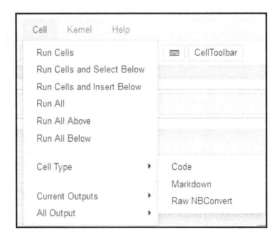

- **Run Cells**: Runs all of the cells in the notebook
- **Run Cells and Select Below**: Runs cells and selects all of the cells below the current
- **Run Cells and Insert Below**: Runs cells and adds a blank cell
- **Run All**: Runs all of the cells
- **Run All Above**: Runs all of the cells above the current
- **Run All Below**: Runs all of the cells below the current
- **Cell Type**: Changes the type of the selected cell(s) to:
    - **Code**: this is the default—the cell would expect to have language statements
    - **Markdown**: The cell contains HTML markdown,-typically used to display the notebook in the best manner (as it is a website, so has all of HTML available to it)
    - **Raw NBConvert**: This is an internal Jupyter format, basically plain text
- **Current Outputs**: Whether to clear or continue the outputs from the cells
- **All Output**

Kernel menu

The **Kernel** menu is used to control the underlying language engine used by the notebook. The menu choices are as follows. I think many of the choices in this menu are used very little:

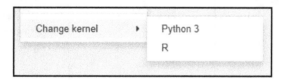

- **Interrupt**: Momentarily stops the underlying language engine and then lets it continue
- **Restart**: Restarts the underlying language engine
- **Restart & Clear Output**
- **Restart & Run All**

- **Reconnect**: If you were to interrupt the kernel, you would then need to reconnect to start running again
- **Change kernel**: Changes the language used in this notebook to one available in your installation

Help menu

The help menu displays the help options for Jupyter and language context choices. For example, in our Python notebook we see choices for common Python libraries that may be used:

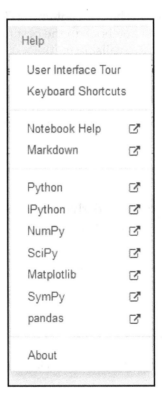

Icon toolbar

Just below the regular menu is an icon toolbar with many of the commonly used menu items for faster use, as seen in this view:

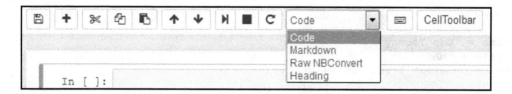

The icons correspond to the previous menu choices (listed in order of appearance):

- File/Save the current notebook
- Insert cell below
- Cut current cells
- Copy the current cells
- Paste cells below
- Move selected cells up
- Move selected cells down
- Run from selected cells down
- Interrupt the kernel
- Restart kernel
- List of formats we can apply to the current cells
- An icon to open a command palette with descriptive names
- An icon to open the cell toolbar

How does it look when we execute scripts?

If we were to provide a name for the notebook, enter a simple Python script, and execute the notebook cells, we would see a display like this:

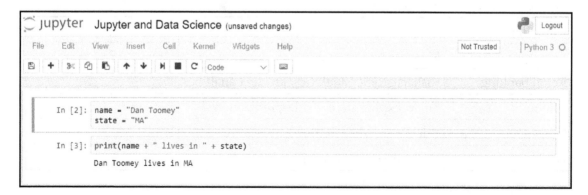

The script is:

```
name = "Dan Toomey"
state = "MA"
print(name + " lives in " + state)
```

We assign a value to the name and state variables and then print them out.

If you notice, I have placed the statements into two different cells. This is just for readability. They could all be in the same cell or three different cells.

There are line numbers assigned to each cell. The numbering always starts at 1 for the first cell, then as you move cells around the numbering may grow (as you can see the first cell is labeled cell 2 in the display).

Below the second cell, we have non-editable display results. Jupyter always displays any corresponding output of a cell just below. This could include error information as well.

Industry data science usage

This book is about Jupyter and data science. We have the introduction to Jupyter. Now, we can look at data science practices and then see how the two concepts work together.

Data science is used in many industries. It is interesting to note the predominant technologies involved and algorithms used by industry. We can see the same technologies available within Jupyter.

Some of the industries that are larger users of data science include:

Industry	Larger data science use	Technology/algorithms
Finance	Hedge funds	Python
Gambling	Establish odds	R
Insurance	Measure and price risk	Domino (R)
Retail banking	Risk, customer analytics, product analytics	R
Mining	Smart exploration, yield optimization	Python
Consumer products	Pricing and distribution	R
Healthcare	Drug discovery and trials	Python

All of these data science investigations could be done in Jupyter, as the languages used are fully supported.

Real life examples

In this section we see several examples taken from current industry focus and apply them in Jupyter to ensure its utility.

Finance, Python - European call option valuation

There is an example of this at `https://www.safaribooksonline.com/library/view/python-for-finance/9781491945360/ch03.html` which is taken from the book *Python for Finance* by Yves Hilpisch. The model used is fairly standard for finance work.

We want to arrive at the theoretical value of a call option. A call option is the right to buy a security, such as IBM stock, at a specific (strike) price within a certain time frame. The option is priced based on the riskiness or volatility of the security in relation to the strike price and current price. The example uses a European option which can only be exercised at maturity-this simplifies the problem set.

The example is using Black-Scholes model for option valuation where we have:

- Initial stock index level $S_0 = 100$
- Strike price of the European call option $K = 105$
- Time-to-maturity $T = 1\ year$
- Constant, riskless short rate $r = 5\%$
- Constant volatility $\sigma = 20\%$

These elements make up the following formula:

$$St = S_0 \exp\left(\left(r - 1/2\sigma^2\right)T + \sigma\sqrt{(T)}\,z\right)$$

The algorithm used is as follows:

1. Draw *I* (pseudo) random numbers from the standard normal distribution.
2. Calculate all resulting index levels at maturity $S_T(i)$ for given $z(i)$ in the previous equation. Calculate all inner values of the option at maturity as $h_T(i) = \max(S_T(i) - K,0)$.
3. Estimate the option present value via the Monte Carlo estimator given in the following equation:

$$C0 \text{ approximates as } e^{-rT}\, 1/I \sum hT(i)$$

The script is as follows. We use numpy for the intense mathematics used. The rest of the coding is typical:

```
from numpy import *
# set parameters
S0 = 100.
K = 105.
T = 1.0
r = 0.05
sigma = 0.2
# how many samples we are using
I = 100000
random.seed(103)
z = random.standard_normal(I)
ST = S0 * exp((r - 0.5 * sigma ** 2) * T + sigma * sqrt(T) * z)
hT = maximum(ST - K, 0)
C0 = exp(-r * T) * sum(hT) / I
# tell user results
print ("Value of the European Call Option %5.3f" % C0)
```

The results under Jupyter are as shown in the following screenshot:

```
In [1]:  #European Option Pricing
         from numpy import *

         # set parameters
         S0 = 100.
         K = 105.
         T = 1.0
         r = 0.05
         sigma = 0.2

         # how many samples we are using
         I = 100000

         random.seed(103)
         z = random.standard_normal(I)
         ST = S0 * exp((r - 0.5 * sigma ** 2) * T + sigma * sqrt(T) * z)
         hT = maximum(ST - K, 0)
         C0 = exp(-r * T) * sum(hT) / I

         # tell user results
         print("Value of the European Call Option %5.3f" % C0)

         Value of the European Call Option 8.071
```

The 8.071 value corresponds with the published expected value *8.019* due to variance in the random numbers used. (I am seeding the random number generator to have reproducible results).

Finance, Python - Monte Carlo pricing

Another algorithm in popular use is Monte Carlo simulation. In Monte Carlo, as the name of the gambling resort implies, we simulate a number of chances taken in a scenario where we know the percentage outcomes of the different results, but do not know exactly what will happen in the next N chances. We can see this model being used at http://www.codeandfinance.com/pricing-options-monte-carlo.html. In this example, we are using Black-Scholes again, but in a different direct method where we see individual steps.

The coding is as follows. The Python coding style for Jupyter is slightly different than used directly in Python, as you can see by the changed imports near the top of the code. Rather than just pulling in the functions you want from a library, you pull in the entire library and the coding uses what is needed:

```
import datetime
import random # import gauss
import math #import exp, sqrt
random.seed(103)
def generate_asset_price(S,v,r,T):
    return S * exp((r - 0.5 * v**2) * T + v * sqrt(T) * gauss(0,1.0))
def call_payoff(S_T,K):
    return max(0.0,S_T-K)
S = 857.29 # underlying price
v = 0.2076 # vol of 20.76%
r = 0.0014 # rate of 0.14%
T = (datetime.date(2013,9,21) - datetime.date(2013,9,3)).days / 365.0
K = 860.
simulations = 90000
payoffs = []
discount_factor = math.exp(-r * T)
for i in xrange(simulations):
    S_T = generate_asset_price(S,v,r,T)
    payoffs.append(
        call_payoff(S_T, K)
    )
price = discount_factor * (sum(payoffs) / float(simulations))
print ('Price: %.4f' % price)
```

The results under Jupyter are shown as follows:

```
In [1]:  #Monte Carlo Pricing
         import datetime
         import random # import gauss
         import math #import exp, sqrt

         random.seed(103)

         def generate_asset_price(S,v,r,T):
             return S * math.exp((r - 0.5 * v**2) * T + v * math.sqrt(T) * random.gauss(0,1.0))

         def call_payoff(S_T,K):
             return max(0.0,S_T-K)

         S = 857.29 # underlying price
         v = 0.2076 # vol of 20.76%
         r = 0.0014 # rate of 0.14%
         T = (datetime.date(2013,9,21) - datetime.date(2013,9,3)).days / 365.0
         K = 860.
         simulations = 90000
         payoffs = []
         discount_factor = math.exp(-r * T)

         for i in range(simulations):
             S_T = generate_asset_price(S,v,r,T)
             payoffs.append(
                 call_payoff(S_T, K)
             )

         price = discount_factor * (sum(payoffs) / float(simulations))
         print('Price: %.4f' % price)

         Price: 14.4452
```

The result price of 14.4452 is close to the published value *14.5069*.

Gambling, R - betting analysis

Some of the gambling games are really coin flips, with 50/50 chances of success. Along those lines we have coding from http://forumserver.twoplustwo.com/25/probability/ flipping-coins-getting-3-row-1233506/ that determines the probability of a series of heads or tails in a coin flip, with a trigger that can be used if you know the coin/game is biased towards one result or the other.

We have the following script:

```
###############################################
# Biased/unbiased  recursion of heads OR tails
###############################################
import numpy as np
import math

N = 14      # number of flips
m = 3       # length of run (must be  > 1 and <= N/2)
p = 0.5   # P(heads)

prob = np.repeat(0.0,N)
h = np.repeat(0.0,N)
t = np.repeat(0.0,N)

h[m] = math.pow(p,m)
t[m] = math.pow(1-p,m)
prob[m] = h[m] + t[m]

for n in range(m+1,2*m):
  h[n] = (1-p)*math.pow(p,m)
  t[n] = p*math.pow(1-p,m)
  prob[n] = prob[n-1] + h[n] + t[n]


for n in range(2*m,N):
  h[n] = ((1-p) - t[n-m] - prob[n-m-1]*(1-p))*math.pow(p,m)
  t[n] = (p - h[n-m] - prob[n-m-1]*p)*math.pow(1-p,m)
  prob[n] = prob[n-1] + h[n] + t[n]

prob[N-1]
```

The preceding code produces the following output in Jupyter:

```
In [11]:  import numpy as np
          import math

          N = 14      # number of flips
          m = 3       # length of run (must be > 1 and <= N/2)
          p = 0.5   # P(heads)

          prob = np.repeat(0.0,N)
          h = np.repeat(0.0,N)
          t = np.repeat(0.0,N)

          h[m] = math.pow(p,m)
          t[m] = math.pow(1-p,m)
          prob[m] = h[m] + t[m]

          for n in range(m+1,2*m):
            h[n] = (1-p)*math.pow(p,m)
            t[n] = p*math.pow(1-p,m)
            prob[n] = prob[n-1] + h[n] + t[n]


          for n in range(2*m,N):
            h[n] = ((1-p) - t[n-m] - prob[n-m-1]*(1-p))*math.pow(p,m)
            t[n] = (p - h[n-m] - prob[n-m-1]*p)*math.pow(1-p,m)
            prob[n] = prob[n-1] + h[n] + t[n]

          prob[N-1]

Out[11]:  0.907958984375
```

We end up with the probability of getting three heads in a row with an unbiased game. In this case, there is a 92% chance (within the range of tests we have run 14 flips).

Insurance, R - non-life insurance pricing

We have an example of using R to come up with the pricing for non-life products, specifically mopeds, at http://www.cybaea.net/journal/2012/03/13/R-code-for-Chapter-2-of-Non_Life-Insurance-Pricing-with-GLM/. The code first creates a table of the statistics available for the product line, then compares the pricing to actual statistics in use.

The first part of the code that accumulates the data is as follows:

```
con <- url("http://www2.math.su.se/~esbj/GLMbook/moppe.sas")
data <- readLines(con, n = 200L, warn = FALSE, encoding = "unknown")
close(con)
## Find the data range
```

```
data.start <- grep("^cards;", data) + 1L
data.end   <- grep("^;", data[data.start:999L]) + data.start - 2L
table.1.2  <- read.table(text = data[data.start:data.end],
                         header = FALSE,
                         sep = "",
                         quote = "",
   col.names = c("premiekl", "moptva", "zon", "dur",
                 "medskad", "antskad", "riskpre", "helpre", "cell"),
                         na.strings = NULL,
                         colClasses = c(rep("factor", 3), "numeric",
                                        rep("integer", 4), "NULL"),
                                        comment.char = "")
rm(con, data, data.start, data.end)
# Remainder of Script adds comments/descriptions
comment(table.1.2) <-
  c("Title: Partial casco moped insurance from Wasa insurance, 1994--1999",
    "Source: http://www2.math.su.se/~esbj/GLMbook/moppe.sas",
    "Copyright: http://www2.math.su.se/~esbj/GLMbook/")
## See the SAS code for this derived field
table.1.2$skadfre = with(table.1.2, antskad / dur)
## English language column names as comments:
comment(table.1.2$premiekl) <-
  c("Name: Class",
    "Code: 1=Weight over 60kg and more than 2 gears",
    "Code: 2=Other")
comment(table.1.2$moptva)   <-
  c("Name: Age",
    "Code: 1=At most 1 year",
    "Code: 2=2 years or more")
comment(table.1.2$zon)      <-
  c("Name: Zone",
    "Code: 1=Central and semi-central parts of Sweden's three largest
cities",
    "Code: 2=suburbs and middle-sized towns",
    "Code: 3=Lesser towns, except those in 5 or 7",
    "Code: 4=Small towns and countryside, except 5--7",
    "Code: 5=Northern towns",
    "Code: 6=Northern countryside",
    "Code: 7=Gotland (Sweden's largest island)")
comment(table.1.2$dur)      <-
  c("Name: Duration",
    "Unit: year")
comment(table.1.2$medskad)  <-
  c("Name: Claim severity",
    "Unit: SEK")
comment(table.1.2$antskad)  <- "Name: No. claims"
comment(table.1.2$riskpre)  <-
  c("Name: Pure premium",
```

```
      "Unit: SEK")
comment(table.1.2$helpre)    <-
  c("Name: Actual premium",
      "Note: The premium for one year according to the tariff in force 1999",
      "Unit: SEK")
comment(table.1.2$skadfre)   <-
  c("Name: Claim frequency",
      "Unit: /year")
## Save results for later
save(table.1.2, file = "table.1.2.RData")
## Print the table (not as pretty as the book)
print(table.1.2)
```

The resultant first 10 rows of the table are as follows:

	premiekl	moptva	zon	dur	medskad	antskad	riskpre	helpre	skadfre
1	1	1	1	62.9	18256	17	4936	2049	0.27027027
2	1	1	2	112.9	13632	7	845	1230	0.06200177
3	1	1	3	133.1	20877	9	1411	762	0.06761833
4	1	1	4	376.6	13045	7	242	396	0.01858736
5	1	1	5	9.4	0	0	0	990	0.00000000
6	1	1	6	70.8	15000	1	212	594	0.01412429
7	1	1	7	4.4	8018	1	1829	396	0.22727273
8	1	2	1	352.1	8232	52	1216	1229	0.14768532
9	1	2	2	840.1	7418	69	609	738	0.08213308
10	1	2	3	1378.3	7318	75	398	457	0.05441486

Then, we go through each product/statistics to determine whether the pricing for a product is in line with others. Note, the repos = clause on the install.packages statement is a fairly new addition to R:

```
# make sure the packages we want to use are installed
install.packages(c("data.table", "foreach", "ggplot2"), dependencies =
TRUE, repos = "http://cran.us.r-project.org")
# load the data table we need
if (!exists("table.1.2"))
  load("table.1.2.RData")
library("foreach")
## We are looking to reproduce table 2.7 which we start building here,
## add columns for our results.
table27 <-
  data.frame(rating.factor =
              c(rep("Vehicle class", nlevels(table.1.2$premiekl)),
                rep("Vehicle age",   nlevels(table.1.2$moptva)),
                rep("Zone",          nlevels(table.1.2$zon))),
            class =
              c(levels(table.1.2$premiekl),
                levels(table.1.2$moptva),
```

```
                  levels(table.1.2$zon)),
             stringsAsFactors = FALSE)
## Calculate duration per rating factor level and also set the
## contrasts (using the same idiom as in the code for the previous
## chapter). We use foreach here to execute the loop both for its
## side-effect (setting the contrasts) and to accumulate the sums.
# new.cols are set to claims, sums, levels
new.cols <-
  foreach (rating.factor = c("premiekl", "moptva", "zon"),
           .combine = rbind) %do%
{
  nclaims <- tapply(table.1.2$antskad, table.1.2[[rating.factor]], sum)
  sums <- tapply(table.1.2$dur, table.1.2[[rating.factor]], sum)
  n.levels <- nlevels(table.1.2[[rating.factor]])
  contrasts(table.1.2[[rating.factor]]) <-
    contr.treatment(n.levels)[rank(-sums, ties.method = "first"), ]
  data.frame(duration = sums, n.claims = nclaims)
}
table27 <- cbind(table27, new.cols)
rm(new.cols)
#build frequency distribution
model.frequency <-
  glm(antskad ~ premiekl + moptva + zon + offset(log(dur)),
      data = table.1.2, family = poisson)
rels <- coef( model.frequency )
rels <- exp( rels[1] + rels[-1] ) / exp( rels[1] )
table27$rels.frequency <-
    c(c(1, rels[1])[rank(-table27$duration[1:2], ties.method = "first")],
      c(1, rels[2])[rank(-table27$duration[3:4], ties.method = "first")],
      c(1, rels[3:8])[rank(-table27$duration[5:11], ties.method = "first")])
# note the severities involved
model.severity <-
  glm(medskad ~ premiekl + moptva + zon,
      data = table.1.2[table.1.2$medskad > 0, ],
      family = Gamma("log"), weights = antskad)
rels <- coef( model.severity )
rels <- exp( rels[1] + rels[-1] ) / exp( rels[1] )
## Aside: For the canonical link function use
## rels <- rels[1] / (rels[1] + rels[-1])
table27$rels.severity <-
    c(c(1, rels[1])[rank(-table27$duration[1:2], ties.method = "first")],
      c(1, rels[2])[rank(-table27$duration[3:4], ties.method = "first")],
      c(1, rels[3:8])[rank(-table27$duration[5:11], ties.method = "first")])
table27$rels.pure.premium <- with(table27, rels.frequency * rels.severity)
print(table27, digits = 2)
```

The resultant display is as follows:

	rating.factor	class	duration	n.claims	rels.frequency	rels.severity
1	Vehicle class	1	9833	391	1.00	1.00
2	Vehicle class	2	8825	395	0.78	0.55
11	Vehicle age	1	1918	141	1.55	1.79
21	Vehicle age	2	16740	645	1.00	1.00
12	Zone	1	1451	206	7.10	1.21
22	Zone	2	2486	209	4.17	1.07
3	Zone	3	2889	132	2.23	1.07
4	Zone	4	10069	207	1.00	1.00
5	Zone	5	246	6	1.20	1.21
6	Zone	6	1369	23	0.79	0.98
7	Zone	7	148	3	1.00	1.20

	rels.pure.premium
1	1.00
2	0.42
11	2.78
21	1.00
12	8.62
22	4.48
3	2.38
4	1.00
5	1.46
6	0.78
7	1.20

Here, we can see that some vehicle classes (2,6) are priced very low in comparison to statistics for that vehicle where as other are overpriced (12, 22).

Consumer products, R - marketing effectiveness

We take the example from a presentation I made at
www.dantoomeysoftware.com/Using_R_for_Marketing_Research.pptx looking at the effectiveness of different ad campaigns for grape fruit juice.

The code is as follows:

```
#library(s20x)
library(car)

#read the dataset from an existing .csv file
df <- read.csv("C:/Users/Dan/grapeJuice.csv",header=T)

#list the name of each variable (data column) and the first six rows of the
dataset
```

```
head(df)

# basic statistics of the variables
summary(df)

#set the 1 by 2 layout plot window
par(mfrow = c(1,2))

# boxplot to check if there are outliers
boxplot(df$sales,horizontal = TRUE, xlab="sales")

# histogram to explore the data distribution shape
hist(df$sales,main="",xlab="sales",prob=T)
lines(density(df$sales),lty="dashed",lwd=2.5,col="red")

#divide the dataset into two sub dataset by ad_type
sales_ad_nature = subset(df,ad_type==0)
sales_ad_family = subset(df,ad_type==1)

#calculate the mean of sales with different ad_type
mean(sales_ad_nature$sales)
mean(sales_ad_family$sales)

#set the 1 by 2 layout plot window
par(mfrow = c(1,2))

# histogram to explore the data distribution shapes
hist(sales_ad_nature$sales,main="",xlab="sales with nature production theme
ad",prob=T)
lines(density(sales_ad_nature$sales),lty="dashed",lwd=2.5,col="red")

hist(sales_ad_family$sales,main="",xlab="sales with family health caring
theme ad",prob=T)
lines(density(sales_ad_family$sales),lty="dashed",lwd=2.5,col="red")
```

With output (several sections):

(raw data from file, first 10 rows):

	sales	price	ad_type	price_apple	price_cookies
1	222	9.83	0	7.36	8.8
2	201	9.72	1	7.43	9.62
3	247	10.15	1	7.66	8.9
4	169	10.04	0	7.57	10.26
5	317	8.38	1	7.33	9.54
6	227	9.74	0	7.51	9.49

Statistics on the data are as follows:

```
      sales            price           ad_type         price_apple
Min.    :131.0   Min.    : 8.200   Min.    :0.0    Min.    :7.300
1st Qu.:182.5    1st Qu.: 9.585    1st Qu.:0.0     1st Qu.:7.438
Median :204.5    Median : 9.855    Median :0.5     Median :7.580
Mean    :216.7   Mean    : 9.738   Mean    :0.5    Mean    :7.659
3rd Qu.:244.2    3rd Qu.:10.268    3rd Qu.:1.0     3rd Qu.:7.805
Max.    :335.0   Max.    :10.490   Max.    :1.0    Max.    :8.290
price_cookies
Min.    : 8.790
1st Qu.: 9.190
Median : 9.515
Mean    : 9.622
3rd Qu.:10.140
Max.    :10.580
```

The data shows the effectiveness of each campaign. Family sales are more effective:

- *186.666666666667//mean of nature sales*
- *246.666666666667//mean of family sales*

The difference is more pronounced on the histogram displays:

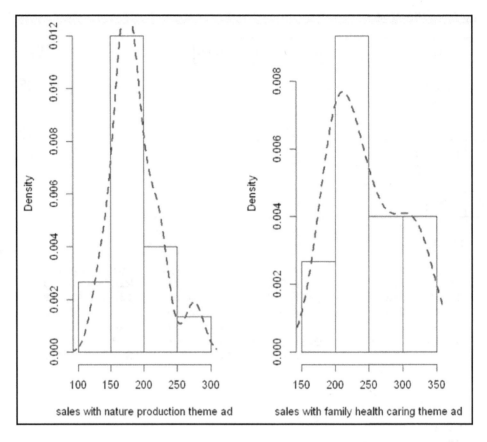

Using Docker with Jupyter

Docker is a mechanism that allows you to have many complete virtual instances of an application in one machine. Docker is used by many software firms to provide a fully scalable implementation of their services, and support as many concurrent users as needed.

Prior mechanisms for dealing with multiple instances shared common resources (such as disk address space). Under Docker, each instance is a complete entity separate from all others.

Implementing Jupyter on a Docker environment allows multiple users to access their own Jupyter instance, without having to worry about interfering with someone else's calculations.

The key feature of Docker is allowing for a variable number of instances of your notebook to be in use at any time. The Docker control system can be set up to create new instances for every user that accesses your notebook. All of this is built-in to Docker without programming; just use the user interface to decide how to create instances.

There are two ways you can use Docker:

- From a public service
- Installing Docker on your machine

Using a public Docker service

There are several services out there. I think they work pretty much the same way: sign up for the service, upload your notebook, monitor usage (the Docker control program tracks usage automatically). For example, if we use `https://hub.docker.com/` we are really using a version repository for our notebook. Versioning is used in software development for tracking changes that are made over time. This also allows for multiple user access privileges as well:

1. First, sign up. This provides authentication to the service vendor.
2. Create a repository—where you will keep your version of the notebook.
3. You will need Docker installed on your machine to pull/push notebooks from/to your repository.

 Installing Docker is operating system dependent. Go to the `https://www.docker.com/` home page for instructions for your machine.

4. Upload (push) your Jupyter image to your repository.
5. Access your notebook in the repository. You can share the address (URL) of your notebook with others under control of Docker, making specific access rights to different users.
6. From then on, it will work just as if it were running locally.

Installing Docker on your machine

Docker on your local machine would only be a precursor to posting on a public Docker service, unless the machine you are installing Docker on is accessible by others.

 Another option is to have Docker installed on your machine. It works exactly like the previous case, except you are managing the Docker image space.

How to share notebooks with others

There are several ways to share Jupyter Notebooks with others:

- Email
- Place onto Google Drive
- Share on GitHub
- Store as HTML on a web server
- Install Jupyter on a web server

Can you email a notebook?

In order to email your notebook, the notebook must be converted to a plain text format, sent as an attachment to the recipient, and then the recipient must convert it back to the 'binary' notebook format.

Email attachments are normally converted to a well-defined **MIME** (**Multi-purpose Internet Mail Extension**) format. There is a program available that converts the notebook format, nb2mail, which converts the notebook to a notebook MIME format. The program is available at https://github.com/nfultz/nb2mail.

Usage is as follows:

- Install nb2mail using pip command (see website)
- Convert your selected notebook to MIME format
- Send to recipient
- The recipient MIME conversion process will store the file in the correct fashion (assuming they have also installed nb2mail)

Sharing a notebook on Google Drive

Google Drive can be used to store your notebook profile information. This might be used when combined with the previous emailing of a notebook to another user. The recipient could use a Google Drive profile that would preclude anyone without the profile information from interacting with the notebook.

You install the python extension (from `https://github.com/jupyter/jupyter-drive`) using `pip` and then `python -m`. From then on, you access the notebooks with the Google Drive profiles, as `ipython notebook -profile <profilename>`.

Sharing on GitHub

GitHub (and others) allow you to place a notebook on their servers that, once there, can be accessed directly using the nbviewer. The server has installed Python (and other language) coding needed to support your notebook. The nbviewer is a read-only use of your notebook, and is not interactive.

The nbviewer is available at `https://github.com/jupyter/nbviewer`. The site includes specific parameters which need to be added to the `ipython notebook` command, such as the command to start the viewer.

Store as HTML on a web server

A built-in feature of notebooks is to export the notebook into different formats. One of those is HTML. In this manner, you could export the notebook into HTML and copy the file(s) onto your web server as changes are made.

The command is `jupyter nbconvert <notebook name>.ipynb --to html`.

Again, this would be a non-interactive, read-only version of your notebook.

Install Jupyter on a web server

Jupyter is deployed as a web application. If you have direct access to a web server, you could install Jupyter on the web server, create notebooks on that web server, and then the notebooks would be available to others that are completely dynamic.

As a web server you also have control over access to the web server so can control who can access your notebook.

This is an advanced interaction that would require working with your webmaster to determine the correct approach.

How can you secure a notebook?

There are two aspects to security in Jupyter Notebooks:

- Making sure only specific users can access your notebook
- Making sure your notebook is not used to host malicious coding

Access control

While many of the uses of Jupyter are solely for educating others, there are instances where the information being accessed is and should remain confidential. Jupyter allows you to put up barriers to entry to your notebook in several manners.

When we identify the user, we are authenticating that user. This is normally done by presenting a login challenge before allowing entry, where the user has to enter a username and password.

If the instance of Jupyter hosting, your notebook is installed on a web server and you can use the web server's access control to limit access to your notebook. Further, most of the vendors that support notebook hosting provide a mechanism to limit access to specific users.

Malicious content

The other aspect of security is to make sure the contents of your notebooks are not malicious. You should make sure your notebook is safe, as follows:

- Ensure that HTML is sanitized (looking for malicious HTML coding and subverting it)
- Do not allow your notebook to execute external JavaScript
- Check cell contents that may be malicious are challenged in a server environment
- Sanitize output of cells so as not to produce unwanted effects on user machines

Summary

In this chapter, we looked into the details of the Jupyter user interface: what objects does it work with, what actions can be taken by Jupyter, what does the display tell us about the data, and what tools are available? Next, we looked at some real-life examples from industry showing R and Python coding from several industries. Then we saw some of the ways to share our notebook with other users and, correspondingly, how to protect our notebook with different security mechanisms.

In the next chapter, we will see how far we can go using Python in a Jupyter Notebook.

Working with Analytical Data on Jupyter

2

Jupyter does none of the heavy lifting for analyzing data: all the work is done by programs written in a selected language. Jupyter provides the framework to run a variety of programming language modules. So, we have a choice how we analyze data in Jupyter.

A popular choice for data analysis programming is Python. Jupyter does have complete support for Python programming. We will look at a variety of programming solutions that might tax such a support system and see how Jupyter fairs.

Data scraping with a Python notebook

A common tool for data analysis is gathering the data from a public source such as a website. Python is adept at scraping websites for data. Here, we look at an example that loads stock price information from Google Finance data.

In particular, given a stock symbol, we want to retrieve the last year of price ranges for that symbol.

One of the pages on the Google Finance site will give the last years' worth of price data for a security company. For example, if we were interested in the price points for **Advanced Micro Devices (AMD)**, we would enter the following URL:

```
https://www.google.com/finance/historical?q=NASDAQ:AMD
```

Here, NASDAQ is the stock exchange that carries the AMD security. On the resultant Google page, there is a table of data points of interest, as seen in the following partial screenshot.

Like many sites that you will be attempting to access, there is a lot of other information on the page as well, like headers and footers and ads, as you can see in the following screenshot. The web pages are built for human readers. Fortunately, Google and these other companies realize you are scraping their data and keep the data in the same format, so you will not have to change scripts.

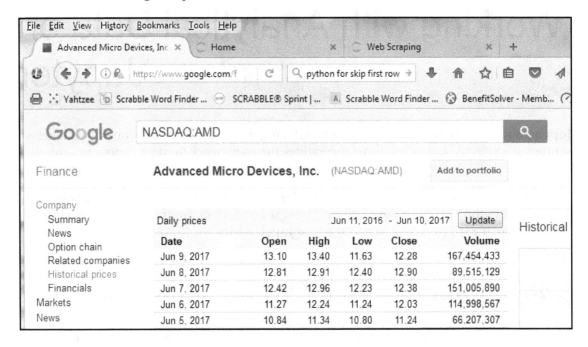

 Be forewarned that you may be blocked from access to a page or an entire site if you were to access the site too frequently. Frequency is a matter for discussion with the particular site you are accessing. Again, the sites know that you are scraping and are okay with that occurring as long as it doesn't interfere with their normal human web traffic.

There is a clear table on that web page. If we look at the underlying HTML used to generate the web page, we find a lot of header, footer, and sidebar information but, more importantly, we find an HTML div tag with the id price_data. Within that div tag, we see an HTML table where each row has the value of date, opening price, high, low, close, and volume for that data as seen on screen.

We can use a standard Python library package, lxml, to load and parse the web page text into constituent HTML Python components that we can work with.

Then, for each day of data, we pull out the columns information and add it to our data list.

Typically, you might run this script once a day and store the newest day's information in your local database for further analysis. In our case, we are just printing out the last day's values on screen.

The Python script used is as follows:

```
from lxml import html
import requests
from time import sleep
# setup the URL for the symbol we are interested in
exchange = "NASDAQ"
ticker = "AMD"
url = "https://www.google.com/finance/historical?q=%s:%s"%(exchange,ticker)
# retrieve the web page
response = requests.get(url)
print ("Retrieving prices for %s from %s"%(ticker,url))
# give it a few seconds in case there is some delay
sleep(3)
# convert the text into an HTML Document
parser = html.fromstring(response.text)
# find the HTML DIV tag that has id 'prices'
price_store = parser.get_element_by_id("prices")
# we will store our price information in the price_data list
price_data = []
# find the HTML TABLE element within the prices DIV
for table in price_store:
    #every row (skip first row headings) of table has
    #  date, open, high, low, close, volume
    for row in table[1:]:
        #store tuples for a day together
        day = {"date":row[0].text.strip('\n'), \
                "open":row[1].text.strip('\n'), \
                "high":row[2].text.strip('\n'), \
                "low":row[3].text.strip('\n'), \
                "close":row[4].text.strip('\n'), \
                "volume":row[5].text.strip('\n')}
        #add day's information to our set
        price_data.append(day)
print ("The last day of pricing information we have is:")
print (price_data[0])
```

Running this script in a Jupyter console, we see results as in the following partial screenshot:

```
In [1]: from lxml import html
        import requests
        from time import sleep

        # setup the URL for the symbol we are interested in
        exchange = "NASDAQ"
        ticker = "AMD"
        url = "https://www.google.com/finance/historical?q=%s:%s"%(exchange,ticker)

        # retrieve the web page
        response = requests.get(url)
        print("Retrieving prices for %s from %s"%(ticker,url))
        # give it a few seconds in case there is some delay
        sleep(3)

        # convert the text into an HTML Document
        parser = html.fromstring(response.text)

        # find the HTML DIV tag that has id 'prices'
        price_store = parser.get_element_by_id("prices")

        # we will store our price information in the price_data list
        price_data = []

        # find the HTML TABLE element within the prices DIV
        for table in price_store:

            #every row (skip first row headings) of table has
            #  date, open, high, low, close, volume
            for row in table[1:]:

                #store tuples for a day together
                day = {"date":row[0].text.strip('\n'), \
                       "open":row[1].text.strip('\n'), \
                       "high":row[2].text.strip('\n'), \
                       "low":row[3].text.strip('\n'), \
                       "close":row[4].text.strip('\n'), \
                       "volume":row[5].text.strip('\n')}

                #add day's information to our set
                price_data.append(day)

        print("The last day of pricing information we have is:")
        print(price_data[0])

        Retrieving prices for AMD from https://www.google.com/finance/historical?q=NASDAQ:AMD
        The last day of pricing information we have is:
        {'date': 'Oct 3, 2017', 'open': '12.73', 'high': '13.48', 'low': '12.70', 'close': '13.42', 'volume':
        '85,174,031'}
```

Using heavy-duty data processing functions in Jupyter

Python has several groups of processing functions that can tax computer system power. Let us use some of these in Jupyter and determine if the functionality performs as expected.

Using NumPy functions in Jupyter

NumPy is a package in Python providing multidimensional arrays and routines for array processing. We bring in the NumPy package using `import * from numpy` statement. In particular, the NumPy package defines the `array` keyword, referencing a NumPy object with extensive functionality.

The NumPy array processing functions run from the mundane, such as `min()` and `max()` functions (which provide the minimum and maximum values over the array dimensions provided), to more interesting utility functions for producing histograms and calculating correlations using the elements of a data frame.

With NumPy, you can manipulate arrays in many ways. For example, we will go over some of these functions with the following scripts, where we will use NumPy to:

- Create an array
- Calculate the max value in the array
- Calculate the min value in the array
- Determine the sum across the second axis

```
# numpy arrays
import numpy as np

# create an array 'a' with 3 3-tuples
a = np.array([[1, 1, 2], [3, 5, 8], [13, 21, 34]])
print("Array contents", a)

# determine the minimum value in array
print("max value = ", a.max())

# max value in array
print("min value = ", a.min())

# sum across the 2nd axis
print("sum across 2nd axis", a.sum(axis = 1))
```

If we transfer this script into a Python notebook, we see a display like the following when we execute the cell:

```
In [1]:  # numpy arrays
         import numpy as np

         # create an array 'a' with 3 3-tuples
         a = np.array([[1, 1, 2], [3, 5, 8], [13, 21, 34]])
         print("Array contents", a)

         # determine the minimum value in array
         print("max value = ", a.max())

         # max value in array
         print("min value = ", a.min())

         # sum across the 2nd axis
         print("sum across 2nd axis", a.sum(axis = 1))

         Array contents [[ 1  1  2]
          [ 3  5  8]
          [13 21 34]]
         max value =  34
         min value =  1
         sum across 2nd axis [ 4 16 68]
```

We can use the use the following script to work over arrays with the more interesting `histogram` and `correlate` functions:

```
import numpy as np
import random

# build up 2 sets of random numbers

# setup empty array 2 columns, 1000 rows
numbers = np.empty([2,1000], int)

# set seed so we can repeat results
random.seed(137)

# populate the array
for num in range(0, 1000):
    numbers[0,num] = random.randint(0, 1000)
    numbers[1,num] = random.randint(0, 1000)

# produce a histogram of the data
(hist, bins) = np.histogram(numbers, bins = 10, range = (0,1000))
print ("Histogram is ",hist)
```

```
# calculate correlation between the 2 columns

corrs = np.correlate(numbers[:,1], numbers[:,2], mode='valid')
print ("Correlation of the two rows is ", corrs)
```

In this script, we are:

- Populating a two-column array with random numbers
- Producing a histogram of the values from both columns within 100 point ranges
- And, finally, determining the correlation between the two columns (which should be a very high correlation)

After entering this script into a Jupyter Notebook and executing the cell, we have an output as follows. It makes sense that the buckets are very close in size:

```
In [1]: # numpy histogram
        import numpy as np
        import random

        # build up 2 sets of random numbers

        # setup empty array 2 columns, 1000 rows
        numbers = np.empty([2,1000], int)

        # set seed so we can repeat results
        random.seed(137)

        # populate the array
        for num in range(0, 1000):
            numbers[0,num] = random.randint(0, 1000)
            numbers[1,num] = random.randint(0, 1000)

        # produce a histogram of the data
        (hist, bins) = np.histogram(numbers, bins = 10, range = (0,1000))
        print("Histogram is ",hist)

        # calculate correlation between the 2 columns

        corrs = np.correlate(numbers[:,1], numbers[:,2], mode='valid')
        print("Correlation of the two rows is ", corrs)

        Histogram is  [197 187 201 221 195 221 183 205 194 196]
        Correlation of the two rows is  [161131]
```

Using pandas in Jupyter

pandas is an open source library of high-performance data analysis tools available in Python. Of particular interest are the functions to:

- Read text files
- Read Excel files
- Read from SQL database
- Operate on data frames

Use pandas to read text files in Jupyter

The most common type of text file that will have analysis data is a CSV file. There are a large variety of datasets available on the internet in this format. We will look at the Titanic survivor data found at https://vincentarelbundock.github.io/Rdatasets/csv/datasets/Titanic.csv.

Like most of the pandas, the function call is very easy to use:

```
import pandas as pd
df = pd.read_csv
('https://vincentarelbundock.github.io/Rdatasets/csv/datasets/Titanic.csv')
print (df.head)
```

However, again like many pandas, there is an extensive set of optional parameters that could be passed into the `read_csv` function, that are defaulted to the most commonly used features so we can write small code like used previously to get our work done. Some of the additional parameters we could use allow us to:

- Skip rows
- Skip/define column headings
- And change index field(s) (Python always wants to keep a main indexing field within a data frame to speed access)

The resultant script execution under Jupyter is shown in the following screenshot. (Note, I am only printing the first and last 30 rows of the table using the `head` function):

```
In [6]:  import pandas as pd

         df = pd.read_csv('https://vincentarelbundock.github.io/Rdatasets/csv/datasets/Titanic.csv')
         print(df.head)

         <bound method NDFrame.head of        Unnamed: 0                                      Name PC1
         ass  \
         0             1                  Allen, Miss Elisabeth Walton     1st
         1             2                  Allison, Miss Helen Loraine      1st
         2             3              Allison, Mr Hudson Joshua Creighton  1st
         3             4        Allison, Mrs Hudson JC (Bessie Waldo Daniels)  1st
         4             5                 Allison, Master Hudson Trevor     1st
```

Use pandas to read Excel files in Jupyter

Similarly, we can load Microsoft Excel files just as easily. For example, the Excel file for the same Titanic dataset is available at `vandebilt.edu` (full link in following script). We have the following script:

```
import pandas as pd
df =
pd.read_excel('http://biostat.mc.vanderbilt.edu/wiki/pub/Main/DataSets/tita
nic3.xls')
print (df.head)
```

There is also an extensive set of optional parameters for reading Excel files as well, for example:

- Select the sheet within the excel file to read
- Skip rows
- Specify the handling of NA values

The resultant flow under Jupyter is as follows. The dataset looks very similar to the prior CSV file read in.

```
In [7]:  import pandas as pd

         df = pd.read_excel('http://biostat.mc.vanderbilt.edu/wiki/pub/Main/DataSets/titanic3.xls')
         print(df.head)

         <bound method NDFrame.head of        pclass   survived
         ame  \
         0         1        1                          Allen, Miss. Elisabeth Walton
         1         1        1                          Allison, Master. Hudson Trevor
         2         1        0                          Allison, Miss. Helen Loraine
         3         1        0               Allison, Mr. Hudson Joshua Creighton
         4         1        0         Allison, Mrs. Hudson J C (Bessie Waldo Daniels)
         5         1        1                                 Anderson, Mr. Harry
```

Using pandas to work with data frames

Once we have a data frame available, there are several pandas available to further process the data. We will look at pandas to:

- groupby function
- Manipulate the columns
- Calculate outliers

Using the groupby function in a data frame

The groupby function can be used to group (and count) the number of records in a data frame that meet your criteria.

Continuing with our Titanic dataset, we can use groupby to count the number of people by age.

We can use the following script:

```
# read in the titanic data set
import pandas as pd
df =
pd.read_excel('http://biostat.mc.vanderbilt.edu/wiki/pub/Main/DataSets/tita
nic3.xls')
# extract just the age column to its own dataset,
# group by the age, and
# add a count for each age
ages = df[['age']].groupby('age')['age'].count()
print (ages)
```

The resultant display under Jupyter is as follows. I had not realized there were so many babies on board.

```
In [9]:  import pandas as pd

         df = pd.read_excel('http://biostat.mc.vanderbilt.edu/wiki/pub/Main/DataSets/titanic3.xls')

         ages = df[['age']].groupby('age')['age'].count()

         print(ages)

         age
         0.1667     1
         0.3333     1
         0.4167     1
         0.6667     1
         0.7500     3
         0.8333     3
         0.9167     2
         1.0000    10
         2.0000    12
```

Manipulating columns in a data frame

An interesting column manipulation is to sort. We can sort the prior age count data to determine the most common ages for travelers on the boat using the `sort_values` function.

The script is as follows:

```
import pandas as pd
df =
pd.read_excel('http://biostat.mc.vanderbilt.edu/wiki/pub/Main/DataSets/tita
nic3.xls')
# the [[]] syntax extracts the column(s) into a new dataframe
# we groupby the age column, and
# apply a count to the age column
ages = df[['age']].groupby('age')['age'].count()
print("The most common ages")
print (ages.sort_values(ascending=False))
```

The resultant Jupyter display is as follows. From the data, there were many younger travelers on board. In light of this, it makes more sense why there were so many babies as well.

```
In [10]:  import pandas as pd

          df = pd.read_excel('http://biostat.mc.vanderbilt.edu/wiki/pub/Main/DataSets/titanic3.xls')

          ages = df[['age']].groupby('age')['age'].count()

          print("The most common ages")
          print(ages.sort_values(ascending=False))

          The most common ages
          age
          24.0000    47
          22.0000    43
          21.0000    41
          30.0000    40
          18.0000    39
          25.0000    34
```

Calculating outliers in a data frame

We can calculate outliers using standard calculations as to whether the absolute value of the difference from the mean value is greater than 1.96 times the standard deviation. (This assumes a normal Gaussian distribution of the data).

For example, using the same Titanic dataset loaded previously, we can determine which passengers were outliers based on age.

The Python script is as follows:

```
import pandas as pd

df =
pd.read_excel('http://biostat.mc.vanderbilt.edu/wiki/pub/Main/DataSets/tita
nic3.xls')

# compute mean age
df['x-Mean'] = abs(df['age'] - df['age'].mean())

# 1.96 times standard deviation for age
df['1.96*std'] = 1.96*df['age'].std()

# this age is an outlier if abs difference > 1.96 times std dev
df['Outlier'] = abs(df['age'] - df['age'].mean()) > 1.96*df['age'].std()

# print (results)
```

```
print ("Dataset dimensions", df.count)
print ("Number of age outliers", df.Outlier.value_counts()[True])
```

And under Jupyter the results show as:

```
Number of age outliers 65
```

So, given there were about 1,300 passengers, we have about 5% outliers, which means that there may be a normal distribution of the ages.

Using SciPy in Jupyter

SciPy is an open source library for mathematics, science and, engineering. With such a wide scope, there are many areas we can explore using SciPy:

- Integration
- Optimization
- Interpolation
- Fourier transforms
- Linear algebra
- There are several other intense sets of functionality as well, such as signal processing

Using SciPy integration in Jupyter

A standard mathematical process is integrating an equation. SciPy accomplishes this using a callback function to iteratively calculate out the integration of your function. For example, suppose that we wanted to determine the integral of the following equation:

$$\int 2\,pi + 1$$

We would use a script like the following. We are using the definition of *pi* from the standard math package.

```
from scipy.integrate import quad
import math

def integrand(x, a, b):
    return a*math.pi + b
```

```
a = 2
b = 1
quad(integrand, 0, 1, args=(a,b))
```

Again, this coding is very clean and simple, yet almost impossible to do in many languages. Running this script in Jupyter we see the results quickly:

```
In [5]:  from scipy.integrate import quad
         import math

         def integrand(x, a, b):
             return a*math.pi + b

         a = 2
         b = 1
         quad(integrand, 0, 1, args=(a,b))

Out[5]:  (7.283185307179586, 8.08596002064242e-14)
```

I was curious how the `integrand` function is used during the execution. I am using this to exercise a call back function. To see this work, I added some debugging information to the script where we count how many iterations occur and what display the values called each time:

```
from scipy.integrate import quad
import math

counter = 0
def integrand(x, a, b):
    global counter
    counter = counter + 1
    print ('called with x=',x,'a = ',a,'b = ', b)
    return a*math.pi + b

a = 2
b = 1
print(quad(integrand, 0, 1, args=(a,b)))
print(counter)
```

We are using a counter at the global level, hence when referencing inside the `integrand` function we use the `global` keyword. Otherwise, Python assumes it is a local variable to the function.

The results are as follows:

```
In [6]:  from scipy.integrate import quad
         import math

         counter = 0
         def integrand(x, a, b):
             global counter
             counter = counter + 1
             print('called with x=',x,'a = ',a,'b = ', b)
             return a*math.pi + b

         a = 2
         b = 1
         I = quad(integrand, 0, 1, args=(a,b))
         print(I)
         print(counter)

called with x= 0.5 a =  2 b =  1
called with x= 0.013046735741414128 a =  2 b =  1
called with x= 0.9869532642585859 a =  2 b =  1
called with x= 0.06746831665550773 a =  2 b =  1
called with x= 0.9325316833444923 a =  2 b =  1
called with x= 0.16029521585048778 a =  2 b =  1
called with x= 0.8397047841495122 a =  2 b =  1
called with x= 0.2833023029353764 a =  2 b =  1
called with x= 0.7166976970646236 a =  2 b =  1
called with x= 0.4255628305091844 a =  2 b =  1
called with x= 0.5744371694908156 a =  2 b =  1
called with x= 0.002171418487095955 a =  2 b =  1
called with x= 0.997828581512904 a =  2 b =  1
called with x= 0.03492125432214588 a =  2 b =  1
called with x= 0.9650787456778541 a =  2 b =  1
called with x= 0.109591136706791155 a =  2 b =  1
called with x= 0.8904088632932085 a =  2 b =  1
called with x= 0.21862143266569767 a =  2 b =  1
called with x= 0.7813785673343023 a =  2 b =  1
called with x= 0.35280356864926987 a =  2 b =  1
called with x= 0.6471964313507301 a =  2 b =  1
(7.283185307179586, 8.085960002064242e-14)
21
```

The function was called 21 times to narrow down the solution.

Using SciPy optimization in Jupyter

With optimization, we are looking to determine a maximum or minimum value of a function over several variables. So, let's use an equation with an interesting curve in it:

$$x^4 - x^3 + x^2 + 1$$

If we take that curve and plot it to see if there is an apparent minimum value, we can use a script like the following that generates a plot as the result. (The `%mathplotlib inline` makes the plot appear inline of the Jupyter session, rather than creating the plot in a new window.)

```
%matplotlib inline
from scipy import optimize
import matplotlib.pyplot as plt
import numpy as np

def f(x):
    return x**4 - x**3 + x**2 + 1

x = np.linspace(-100, 50, 100)
plt.plot(x, f(x));
```

Running this script in Jupyter, we see there is a natural minimum at $x = 0$.

Using SciPy interpolation in Jupyter

With interpolation, we are taking a guess at a value for a function given a set of discrete points. For example, suppose that your test results showed something like this:

```
%matplotlib inline
import matplotlib.pyplot as plt

x = [1, 3, 5, 7]
y = [0.5, 0.4, 0.35, 0.29]
plt.plot(x,y)
```

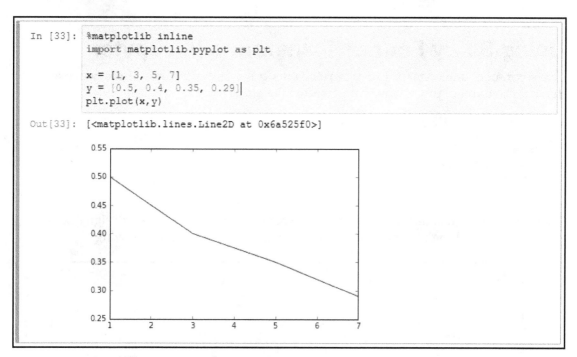

In this case, we could interpolate the result of the function when *x* is 4 using a script like this:

```
from scipy.interpolate import interp1d
g = interp1d(x, y)
print (g(4))
```

This gives us the result of 0.375, which sounds correct.

```
In [3]: from scipy.interpolate import interp1d

        g = interp1d(x, y)

        print(g(4))

        0.375
```

Using SciPy Fourier Transforms in Jupyter

There is a set of functions for **FFT** (**Fourier Transforms**) in SciPy. They are easy to use, given the amount of processing that needs to take place.

We can perform a FFT using coding as follows:

```
from scipy.fftpack import fft
import numpy as np
x = np.array([2.0, 1.0, 2.0, 1.0, 2.0])
fft(x)
```

Here, we have a small dataset to analyze. The data points represent a small signal set we have to evaluate. When taken under Jupyter, we get a display as the following:

```
In [1]: from scipy.fftpack import fft
        import numpy as np

        x = np.array([2.0, 1.0, 2.0, 1.0, 2.0])
        fft(x)

Out[1]: array([ 8.0+0.j        ,  0.5+0.36327126j,  0.5+1.53884177j,
                0.5-1.53884177j,  0.5-0.36327126j])
```

Note that even for this small set of data, the transform operation was busy for several seconds.

We could also use a generated dataset as in this coding:

```
from scipy.fftpack import fft
import numpy as np

# how many points
```

```
n = 100
spacing = 1.0 / 250.0
x = np.linspace(0.0, n*spacing, n)
y = np.sin(30.0 * np.pi * x) + 0.5 * np.sin(7.0 * np.pi * x)
yf = fft(y)
xf = np.linspace(0.0, 1.0/(2.0*spacing), n//2)

#plot the data to get a visual
import matplotlib.pyplot as plt
plt.plot(xf, 2.0/n * np.abs(yf[0:n//2]))
plt.grid()
plt.show()
```

Running this script under Jupyter generates this graphic of the data points in a new screen:

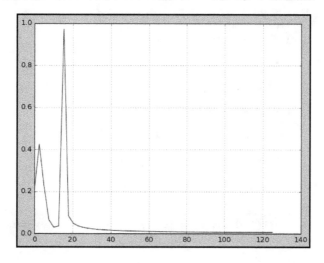

This looks along the lines of what we expected, with a big and small wave in the display.

Using SciPy linear algebra in Jupyter

There is a complete set of linear algebra functions available. For example, we can solve a linear system with steps such as the following:

```
import numpy as np
from scipy import linalg

A = np.array([[1, 1], [2, 3]])
print ("A array")
print (A)
```

```
b = np.array([[1], [2]])
print ("b array")
print (b)

solution = np.linalg.solve(A, b)
print ("solution ")
print (solution)

# validate results
print ("validation of solution (should be a 0 matrix)")
print (A.dot(solution) - b)
```

Here, the output under Jupyter looks like the following:

```
In [1]:  # scipi liner algebra
         import numpy as np
         from scipy import linalg

         A = np.array([[1, 1], [2, 3]])
         print("A array")
         print(A)

         b = np.array([[1], [2]])
         print("b array")
         print(b)

         solution = np.linalg.solve(A, b)
         print("solution ")
         print(solution)

         # validate results
         print("validation of solution (should be a 0 matrix)")
         print(A.dot(solution) - b)

         A array
         [[1 1]
          [2 3]]
         b array
         [[1]
          [2]]
         solution
         [[ 1.]
          [-0.]]
         validation of solution (should be a 0 matrix)
         [[ 0.]
          [ 0.]]
```

We validate the results with the final 0 matrix.

Expanding on panda data frames in Jupyter

There are more functions built-in for working with data frames than we have used so far. If we were to take one of the data frames from a prior example in this chapter, the Titanic dataset from an Excel file, we could use additional functions to help portray and work with the dataset.

As a repeat, we load the dataset using the script:

```
import pandas as pd
df =
pd.read_excel('http://biostat.mc.vanderbilt.edu/wiki/pub/Main/DataSets/tita
nic3.xls')
```

We can then inspect the data frame using the `info` function, which displays the characteristics of the data frame:

```
df.info()
```

```
In [12]: print(df.info())
         <class 'pandas.core.frame.DataFrame'>
         RangeIndex: 1309 entries, 0 to 1308
         Data columns (total 14 columns):
         pclass      1309 non-null int64
         survived    1309 non-null int64
         name        1309 non-null object
         sex         1309 non-null object
         age         1046 non-null float64
         sibsp       1309 non-null int64
         parch       1309 non-null int64
         ticket      1309 non-null object
         fare        1308 non-null float64
         cabin       295 non-null object
         embarked    1307 non-null object
         boat        486 non-null object
         body        121 non-null float64
         home.dest   745 non-null object
         dtypes: float64(3), int64(4), object(7)
         memory usage: 143.2+ KB
         None
```

Some of the interesting points are as follows:

- 1309 entries
- 14 columns
- Not many fields with valid data in the `body` column—most were lost
- Does give a good overview of the types of data involved

We can also use the `describe` function, which gives us a statistical breakdown of the number columns in the data frame.

```
df.describe()
```

This produces the following tabular display:

In [4]:	df.describe()						
Out[4]:		pclass	survived	age	sibsp	parch	fare	body
	count	1309.000000	1309.000000	1046.000000	1309.000000	1309.000000	1308.000000	121.000000
	mean	2.294882	0.381971	29.881135	0.498854	0.385027	33.295479	160.809917
	std	0.837836	0.486055	14.413500	1.041658	0.865560	51.758668	97.696922
	min	1.000000	0.000000	0.166700	0.000000	0.000000	0.000000	1.000000
	25%	2.000000	0.000000	21.000000	0.000000	0.000000	7.895800	72.000000
	50%	3.000000	0.000000	28.000000	0.000000	0.000000	14.454200	155.000000
	75%	3.000000	1.000000	39.000000	1.000000	0.000000	31.275000	256.000000
	max	3.000000	1.000000	80.000000	8.000000	9.000000	512.329200	328.000000

For each numerical column we have:

- Count
- Mean
- Standard deviation
- 25, 50, and 75 percentile points
- Min, max values for the item

We can slice rows of interest using the syntax `df[12:13]`, where the first number (defaults to first row in data frame) is the first row to slice off and the second number (defaults to the last row in the data frame) is the last row to slice off.

Running this slice operation we get the expected results:

```
In [15]: print(df[12:13])

         pclass  survived                              name     sex   age  sibsp  \
     12       1         1  Aubart, Mme. Leontine Pauline  female  24.0      0

         parch    ticket  fare cabin embarked boat  body     home.dest
     12       0  PC 17477  69.3   B35        C    9   NaN  Paris, France
```

Since we are effectively creating a new data frame when we select columns from a data frame, we can then use the `head` function against that as well:

```
In [16]: print(df["age"].head())

     0    29.0000
     1     0.9167
     2     2.0000
     3    30.0000
     4    25.0000
     Name: age, dtype: float64
```

Sorting and filtering data frames in Jupyter/IPython

Data frames automatically allow you to easily sort and filter the dataset involved, using existing functionality within the data frames themselves.

Filtering a data frame

We can select/filter specific rows based on criteria (using the same Titanic data frame):

```
print(df[df.age < 5])
```

This means that we look into the data frame and select the rows where the age of the person is below five years old. (Again, this is creating a new data frame that can be manipulated as needed.)

```
In [5]: print (df[df.age < 5])

        pclass  survived                                 name     sex  \
    1        1         1         Allison, Master. Hudson Trevor    male
    2        1         0         Allison, Miss. Helen Loraine    female
    94       1         1             Dodge, Master. Washington    male
    339      2         1             Becker, Master. Richard F    male
```

If you think about this, you can apply almost any filter to a data frame. Then you can do things like select part of one data frame and combine/join with parts of another data frame. Very quickly, you end up with SQL-like manipulations that can be performed on database tables. With that point of view, you are open to a much wider spectrum of data manipulation than would appear in the base data frame.

Sorting a data frame

Sorting in most languages means re-organizing the dataset that you are working with. In data frames, sorting can be accomplished by selecting another index to access the data frame. All data frames start out with a basic incremental row index built-in by NumPy. You can change the index used to access the data frame and effectively sort the data frame in the manner that you want.

If we look at the display of the (Titanic) data frame, we notice the unnamed first column of ordinal values:

```
In [17]: print(df.head())

        pclass  survived                                               name     sex  \
    0        1         1                        Allen, Miss. Elisabeth Walton  female
    1        1         1                       Allison, Master. Hudson Trevor    male
    2        1         0                         Allison, Miss. Helen Loraine  female
    3        1         0               Allison, Mr. Hudson Joshua Creighton    male
    4        1         0  Allison, Mrs. Hudson J C (Bessie Waldo Daniels)  female
```

If we were to assign another index to use on the data frame, we would sort the data frame by that index. For example:

```
df.set_index('name').head()
```

```
In [10]:  print(df.set_index('name').head())
```

	pclass	survived	sex \
name			
Allen, Miss. Elisabeth Walton	1	1	female
Allison, Master. Hudson Trevor	1	1	male
Allison, Miss. Helen Loraine	1	0	female
Allison, Mr. Hudson Joshua Creighton	1	0	male
Allison, Mrs. Hudson J C (Bessie Waldo Daniels)	1	0	female

Remember, since we have not assigned this new data frame (with the name index) we still have our original data frame intact.

Along the lines of the prior section, there is actually a sorting operation that can be performed against a data frame as well, using the sort_values method. For example, if we were to use the following script:

print(df.sort_values(by='home.dest', ascending=True).head())

This script takes the data frame, sorts it by the home.dest column in ascending order and prints the first five records (in that order)

We would see results as follows:

```
In [12]:  print(df.sort_values(by='home.dest', ascending=True).head())
```

	pclass	survived	name \
222	1	0	Ovies y Rodriguez, Mr. Servando
582	2	1	Watt, Miss. Bertha J
583	2	1	Watt, Mrs. James (Elizabeth "Bessie" Inglis Mi...
298	1	1	Tucker, Mr. Gilbert Milligan Jr
635	3	0	Arnold-Franchi, Mr. Josef

	sex	age	sibsp	parch	ticket	fare	cabin	embarked	boat \
222	male	28.5	0	0	PC 17562	27.7208	D43	C	NaN
582	female	12.0	0	0	C.A. 33595	15.7500	NaN	S	9
583	female	40.0	0	0	C.A. 33595	15.7500	NaN	S	9
298	male	31.0	0	0	2543	28.5375	C53	C	7
635	male	25.0	1	0	349237	17.8000	NaN	S	NaN

	body	home.dest
222	189.0	?Havana, Cuba
582	NaN	Aberdeen / Portland, OR
583	NaN	Aberdeen / Portland, OR
298	NaN	Albany, NY
635	NaN	Altdorf, Switzerland

Summary

In this chapter, we looked at some of the more compute intensive tasks that might be performed in Jupyter. We used Python to scrape a website to gather data for analysis. We used Python NumPy, pandas, and SciPy functions for in-depth computation of results. We went further into pandas and explored manipulating data frames. Lastly, we saw examples of sorting and filtering data frames.

In the next chapter, we will make some predictions and use visualization to validate our predictions.

3
Data Visualization and Prediction

Making predictions is usually precarious. However, there are methods that have been in use that provide some confidence in your results. Under Jupyter, we can use Python and/or R for predictions with readily available functionality.

Make a prediction using scikit-learn

scikit-learn is a machine learning toolset built using Python. Part of the package is supervised learning, where the sample data points have attributes that allow you to assign the data points into separate classes. We use an estimator that assigns a data point to a class and makes predictions as to other data points with similar attributes. In scikit-learn, an estimator provides two functions, `fit()` and `predict()`, providing mechanisms to classify data points and predict classes of other data points, respectively.

As an example, we will be using the housing data from `https://uci.edu/` (I think this is data for the Boston area). There are a number of factors including a price factor.

We will take the following steps:

- We will break up the dataset into a training set and a test set
- From the training set, we will produce a model
- We will then use the model against the test set and evaluate how well our model fits the actual data for predicting housing prices

The attributes in the dataset (in corresponding order in our data frame) are:

CRIM	per capita crime rate by town
ZN	proportion of residential land zoned for lots over 25,000 sq.ft.
INDUS	proportion of non-retail business acres per town
CHAS	Charles River dummy variable (= 1 if tract bounds river; 0 otherwise)
NOX	nitric oxides concentration (parts per 10 million)
RM	average number of rooms per dwelling
AGE	proportion of owner-occupied units built prior to 1940
DIS	weighted distances to five Boston employment centers
RAD	index of accessibility to radial highways
TAX	full-value property-tax rate per $10,000
PTRATIO	pupil-teacher ratio by town
B	*1000(Bk - 0.63)^2 where Bk* is the proportion of black residents by town
LSTAT	% lower status of the population
MEDV	Median value of owner-occupied homes in $1,000's

The following coding is followed by a discussion of the algorithm used and results:

```
#define all the imports we are using
import matplotlib.pyplot as plt
import numpy as np
import pandas as pd
import random
from sklearn import datasets, linear_model
from sklearn.cross_validation import train_test_split
# load the data set
df =
pd.read_table('http://archive.ics.uci.edu/ml/machine-learning-databases/hou
sing/housing.data', sep='\s+')
# add column names
df.columns = ['CRIM', 'ZN', 'INDUS', 'CHAS', 'NOX', \
              'RM', 'AGE', 'DIS', 'RAD', 'TAX', 'PRATIO',\
              'B', 'LSTAT', 'MDEV']
#produce basic statistics to make sure things are lined up
df.head()
```

The results of the `head()` function is the first few rows of the data frame:

	CRIM	ZN	INDUS	CHAS	NOX	RM	AGE	DIS	RAD	TAX	PRATIO	B	LSTA
0	0.02731	0.0	7.07	0	0.469	6.421	78.9	4.9671	2	242.0	17.8	396.90	9.14
1	0.02729	0.0	7.07	0	0.469	7.185	61.1	4.9671	2	242.0	17.8	392.83	4.03
2	0.03237	0.0	2.18	0	0.458	6.998	45.8	6.0622	3	222.0	18.7	394.63	2.94
3	0.06905	0.0	2.18	0	0.458	7.147	54.2	6.0622	3	222.0	18.7	396.90	5.33
4	0.02985	0.0	2.18	0	0.458	6.430	58.7	6.0622	3	222.0	18.7	394.12	5.21

```
df.describe()
```

Similarly, the preceding `describe` statement gives us some quick statistics on the data frame:

	CRIM	ZN	INDUS	CHAS	NOX	RM	AGE
count	505.000000	505.000000	505.000000	505.000000	505.000000	505.000000	505.000(
mean	3.620667	11.350495	11.154257	0.069307	0.554728	6.284059	68.5815{
std	8.608572	23.343704	6.855868	0.254227	0.115990	0.703195	28.1763;
min	0.009060	0.000000	0.460000	0.000000	0.385000	3.561000	2.90000(
25%	0.082210	0.000000	5.190000	0.000000	0.449000	5.885000	45.0000(
50%	0.259150	0.000000	9.690000	0.000000	0.538000	6.208000	77.7000(

When splitting up the dataset between training and test sets, we use random allocation between the two. This gives us an unbiased set of data to work with. However, in order for you to reproduce the results shown here, you need to use the same random seed/starting value. This is why the `random.seed()` call is made. In practice, you would forgo this method call:

```
#we are going to be splitting up the data set 'randomly',
#however we need to reproduce results so set the seed
random.seed(3277)
#split the data into training and testing (25% for testing)
training, testing = train_test_split(df, test_size = 0.25)
#need this step to create an instance of the lreg model
regr = linear_model.LinearRegression()
# Train the model using the training set (MDEV=target)
```

```
training_data = training.drop('MDEV', axis=1)
training_test = training.iloc[:,-1] #training.loc[:,['MDEV']]
#look at coefficients in the model to validate
regr.fit(training_data,training_test)
print('Coefficients: \n', regr.coef_)
'Coefficients: \n', array([
        -1.18763385e-01,    4.19752612e-02,   -1.18584543e-02,
         5.53125252e-01,   -1.19774970e+01,    3.80050180e+00,
        -8.55663104e-03,   -1.46613256e+00,    3.86772585e-01,
        -1.53024705e-02,   -9.55933426e-01,    1.31347272e-02,
        -5.28183554e-01]))
```

Most of these are small numbers, except for a positive correlation with #6 at 3.8 for the number of rooms and a negative correlation with #8 at -1.5 for the distance from the business center. It is interesting how people value being close to work so highly:

```
#split up our test set
testing_data = testing.loc[:,['CRIM', 'ZN', 'INDUS', 'CHAS',\
'NOX', 'RM', 'AGE', 'DIS', 'RAD', 'TAX', 'PRATIO', 'B',\
'LSTAT']]
testing_test = testing[['MDEV']].as_matrix()
#make our prediction
prediction_of_test = regr.predict(testing_data)
# compute MSE
# would usually use the built-in mse function,
# but the test_test and prediction have diff # cols
sum = 0
rows = len(testing_test)
for i in range(rows):
    test = testing_test[i]
    prediction = prediction_of_test[i]
    diff = (test - prediction) ** 2
    sum = sum + diff
mse = sum / rows
print("MSE ", mse)
('MSE ', array([ 23.1571225]))
```

There is an MSE of 23, which seems very low in comparison to the size of the numbers being worked with. Now, let us graph our results to get a good visual of what is going on:

```
%matplotlib inline
#this preceding line is needed to display inline on Jupyter

#plot the tests and predictions
plt.scatter(testing_test, prediction_of_test, color='black')

#draw a line through the middle showing the fit
x0 = min(testing_test)
x1 = max(testing_test)
y0 = min(prediction_of_test)
y1 = max(prediction_of_test)
plt.plot([x0,x1],[y0,y1], color="red")

#add labels
plt.xlabel("Actual Price")
plt.ylabel("Predicted Price")
plt.title("Actual Price vs Predicted Price")

plt.show()
```

Visually, we appear to have a good fit. Most of the data points are aligned with the axis drawn through. There are, as always, a few distinct outliers such as at *20, 50*:

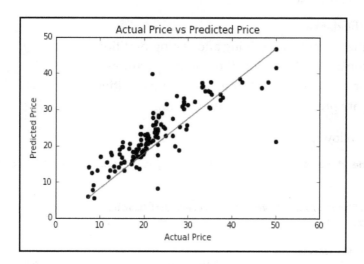

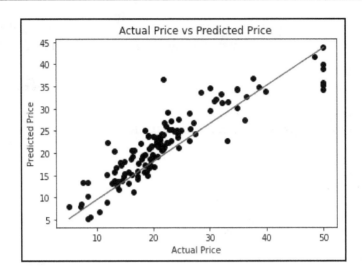

Make a prediction using R

We can perform the same analysis using R in a notebook. The functions are different for the different language, but the functionality is very close.

We use the same algorithm:

- Load the dataset
- Split the dataset into training and testing partitions
- Develop a model based on the training partition
- Use the model to predict from the testing partition
- Compare predicted versus actual testing

The coding is as follows:

```
#load in the data set from uci.edu (slightly different from other housing
model)
housing <-
read.table("http://archive.ics.uci.edu/ml/machine-learning-databases/housin
g/housing.data")

#assign column names
colnames(housing) <- c("CRIM", "ZN", "INDUS", "CHAS", "NOX",
                "RM", "AGE", "DIS", "RAD", "TAX", "PRATIO",
                "B", "LSTAT", "MDEV")
#make sure we have the right data being loaded
```

```
summary(housing)
      CRIM                    ZN                   INDUS                  CHAS
Min.   : 0.00632     Min.   :  0.00      Min.   : 0.46       Min.   :0.00000
1st Qu.: 0.08204     1st Qu.:  0.00      1st Qu.: 5.19       1st Qu.:0.00000
Median : 0.25651     Median :  0.00      Median : 9.69       Median :0.00000
Mean   : 3.61352     Mean   : 11.36      Mean   :11.14       Mean   :0.06917
3rd Qu.: 3.67708     3rd Qu.: 12.50      3rd Qu.:18.10       3rd Qu.:0.00000
Max.   :88.97620     Max.   :100.00      Max.   :27.74       Max.   :1.00000
      NOX                     RM                   AGE                    DIS
Min.   :0.3850       Min.   :3.561       Min.   :  2.90      Min.   : 1.130
1st Qu.:0.4490       1st Qu.:5.886       1st Qu.: 45.02      1st Qu.: 2.100
Median :0.5380       Median :6.208       Median : 77.50      Median : 3.207
Mean   :0.5547       Mean   :6.285       Mean   : 68.57      Mean   : 3.795
3rd Qu.:0.6240       3rd Qu.:6.623       3rd Qu.: 94.08      3rd Qu.: 5.188
Max.   :0.8710       Max.   :8.780       Max.   :100.00      Max.   :12.127
...
```

Make sure the dataset is in the right order for our modeling.

```
housing <- housing[order(housing$MDEV),]

#check if there are any relationships between the data items
plot(housing)
```

The data display, shown as follows, plots every variable against every other variable in the dataset. I am looking to see if there are any nice 45 degree 'lines' showing great symmetry between the variables, with the idea that maybe we should remove one as the other suffices as a contributing factor. The interesting items are:

- CHAS: Charles River access, but that is a binary value.
- LSTAT (lower status population) and MDEV (price) have an inverse relationship—but price will not be a factor.
- NOX (smog) and DIST (distance to work) have an inverse relationship. I think we want that.

- Otherwise, there doesn't appear to be any relationship between the data items:

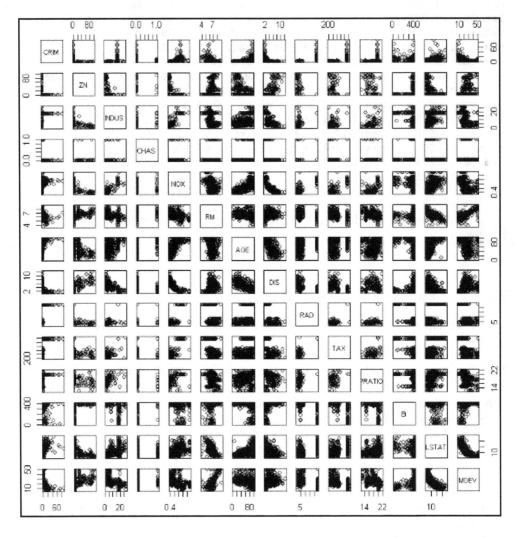

We go about forcing the seed, as before, to be able to reproduce results. We then split the data into training and testing partitions made with the `createDataPartitions` function. We can then train our model and test the resultant model for validation:

```
#force the random seed so we can reproduce results
set.seed(133)

#caret package has function to partition data set
```

```
library(caret)
trainingIndices <- createDataPartition(housing$MDEV, p=0.75, list=FALSE)
#break out the training vs testing data sets
housingTraining <- housing[trainingIndices,]
housingTesting <- housing[-trainingIndices,]
#note their sizes
nrow(housingTraining)
nrow(housingTesting)
#note there may be warning messages to update packages
381
125


#build a linear model
linearModel <- lm(MDEV ~ CRIM + ZN + INDUS + CHAS + NOX + RM + AGE +
                  DIS + RAD + TAX + PRATIO + B + LSTAT,
data=housingTraining)
summary(linearModel)
Call:
lm(formula = MDEV ~ CRIM + ZN + INDUS + CHAS + NOX + RM + AGE +
    DIS + RAD + TAX + PRATIO + B + LSTAT, data = housingTraining)

Residuals:
    Min      1Q   Median      3Q     Max
-15.8448 -2.7961 -0.5602  2.0667 25.2312

Coefficients:
            Estimate Std. Error t value Pr(>|t|)
(Intercept) 36.636334   5.929753   6.178 1.72e-09 ***
CRIM        -0.134361   0.039634  -3.390 0.000775 ***
ZN           0.041861   0.016379   2.556 0.010997 *
INDUS        0.029561   0.068790   0.430 0.667640
CHAS         3.046626   1.008721   3.020 0.002702 **
NOX        -17.620245   4.610893  -3.821 0.000156 ***
RM           3.777475   0.484884   7.790 6.92e-14 ***
AGE          0.003492   0.016413   0.213 0.831648
DIS         -1.390157   0.235793  -5.896 8.47e-09 ***
RAD          0.309546   0.078496   3.943 9.62e-05 ***
TAX         -0.012216   0.004323  -2.826 0.004969 **
PRATIO      -0.998417   0.155341  -6.427 4.04e-10 ***
B            0.009745   0.003300   2.953 0.003350 **
LSTAT       -0.518531   0.060614  -8.555 3.26e-16 ***
---
Signif. codes:  0 '***' 0.001 '**' 0.01 '*' 0.05 '.' 0.1 ' ' 1

Residual standard error: 4.867 on 367 degrees of freedom
Multiple R-squared:  0.7327,   Adjusted R-squared:  0.7233
F-statistic:  77.4 on 13 and 367 DF,  p-value: < 2.2e-16
```

It is interesting that this model also picked up on a high premium for Charles River views affecting the price. Also, like that, this model provides `p-value` (good confidence in the model):

```
# now that we have a model, make a prediction
predicted <- predict(linearModel,newdata=housingTesting)
summary(predicted)

#visually compare prediction to actual
plot(predicted, housingTesting$MDEV)
```

It looks like a pretty good correlation, very close to a 45 degree mapping. The exception is that the predicted values are a little higher than actuals:

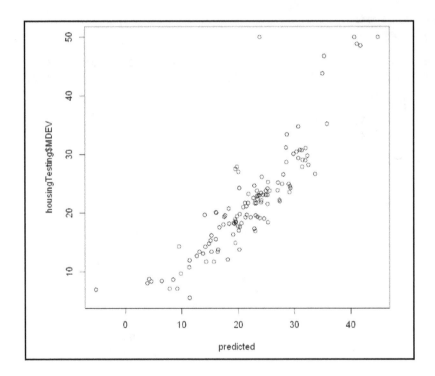

Interactive visualization

There is a Python package, Bokeh, that can be used to generate a figure in your notebook where the user can interact and change the figure.

In this example, I am using the same data from the histogram example later in this chapter (also included in the file set for this chapter) to display an interactive Bokeh histogram.

The coding is as follows:

```
from bokeh.io import show, output_notebook
from bokeh.charts import Histogram
import numpy as np
import pandas as pd
# this step is necessary to have display inline in a notebook
output_notebook()
# load the counts from other histogram example
from_counts = np.load("from_counts.npy")
# convert array to a dataframe for Histogram
df = pd.DataFrame({'Votes':from_counts})
# make sure dataframe is working correctly
print(df.head())
    Votes
0      23
1      29
2      23
3     302
4      24
# display the Bokeh histogram
hist = Histogram(from_counts, \
title="How Many Votes Made By Users", \
bins=12)
show(hist)
```

We can see the histogram displayed as follows. There is little being done automatically to clean up the graph, such as move counters around or the uninteresting axes labels. I assume there are options with the `Histogram` function that would allow further changes:

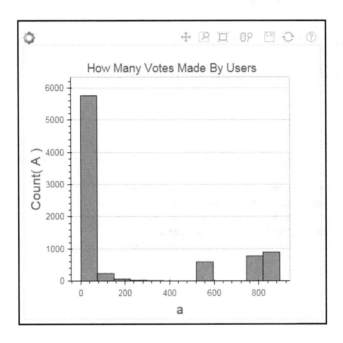

Notice the widgets across the top of the image:

- On the left side is a Bokeh icon
- On the right side are icons for:
  - Moving the image to another portion of the screen
  - Magnifying
  - Resizing
  - Wheel zoom-slide wheel to zoom in/out
  - Save the image to disk
  - Refresh the image
  - Interactive help on Bokeh functions

Plotting using Plotly

Plotly is an interesting mix. It is a subscription website that provides significant data analysis graphing functionality. You can use the free version of the software, but you still need to log in with credentials to use it. The graphics functions are available in a variety of languages from Node.js to Python and the like.

Further, the graphics generated are available in Plotly and in your local notebook. If you mark the graphic as public, then you can access it from the notebook, just like any other graphic over the internet. Similarly, as a web graphic, you can select from the display and save locally as needed.

In this example, we use the voting histogram again, but using Plotly's capabilities.

The script becomes the following:

```
import plotly
import plotly.graph_objs as go
import plotly.plotly as py
import pandas as pd
import numpy as np

#once you set credentials they are stored in local space and referenced
automatically
#you need to subscribe to the site to get the credentials
#the api key would need to be replaced with your key
#plotly.tools.set_credentials_file(username='DemoAccount',
api_key='lr17zw81')

#we are generating a graphic that anyone can see it
plotly.tools.set_config_file(world_readable=True, sharing='public')

# load voting summary from other project
from_counts = np.load("from_counts.npy")
print(from_counts.shape)
(6110,)

#plotly expects a list in a data block
from_count_list = []
for from_count in from_counts:
    from_count_list.append(from_count)

data = [go.Histogram(x=from_count_list)]

# plot on plot.ly site
py.iplot(data, filename='basic histogram')
```

I think this is one of the nicer renderings that I have seen for a histogram using the out-of-the-box options/settings. We have the same histogram we had seen previously, just displayed using more eye-appealing attributes:

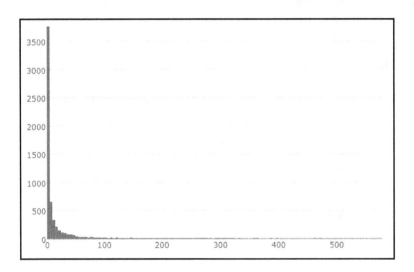

Creating a human density map

I had originally planned on producing a worldwide human density map, but the graphics available don't allow for setting the color of each country. So, I built a density map for the United States.

The algorithm is:

1. Obtain graphic shapes for each of the states.
2. Obtain the density for each state.
3. Decide on a color range and apply the lowest density to one end of the range and the highest to the other end.
4. For each state:
   - Determine it's density
   - Lookup that density value in the range and select a color
   - Draw the state

This is coded with the following (comments embedded as the code proceeds):

```
%matplotlib inline
import matplotlib.pyplot as plt
from mpl_toolkits.basemap import Basemap
from matplotlib.patches import Polygon
import pandas as pd
import numpy as np
import matplotlib
# create the map
map = Basemap(llcrnrlon=-119,llcrnrlat=22,urcrnrlon=-64,urcrnrlat=49,
        projection='lcc',lat_1=33,lat_2=45,lon_0=-95)
# load the shapefile, use the name 'states'
# download from
# https://github.com/matplotlib/basemap/tree/master/examples/st99_d00.dbf,shx
,shp
map.readshapefile('st99_d00', name='states', drawbounds=True)
# collect the state names from the shapefile attributes so we can
# look up the shape obect for a state by it's name
state_names = []
for shape_dict in map.states_info:
    state_names.append(shape_dict['NAME'])
ax = plt.gca() # get current axes instance
# load density data drawn from
# https://en.wikipedia.org/wiki/List_of_U.S._states_by_population_density
df = pd.read_csv('states.csv')
print(df.head())
```

```
State          rank density/mi2  density/km2  pop_rank   2015_pop
New Jersey      1      1,218         470         11     8,958,013
Rhode Island    2      1,021         394         43     1,056,298
Massachusetts   3        871         336         15     6,794,422
Connecticut     4        741         286         29     3,590,886
Maryland        5        618         238         19     6,006,401
   land_rank area_mi2    area_km2
0        46    7,354   19,046.80
1        50    1,034    2,678.00
2        45    7,800   20,201.90
3        48    4,842   12,540.70
4        42    9,707   25,141.00
```

```
# determine the range of density values
max_density = -1.0
min_density = -1.0
for index, row in df.iterrows():
    d = row['density/mi2']
    density = float(d.replace(',' , ''))
    if (max_density==-1.0) or (max_density<density):
        max_density = density
    if (min_density==-1.0) or (min_density>density):
```

```
        min_density = density
print('max',max_density)
print('min',min_density)
range_density = max_density - min_density
print(range_density)
('max', 1218.0)
('min', 1.0)
1217.0
# we pick a color for the state density out of color map
cmap = matplotlib.cm.get_cmap('Spectral')
# for each state get the color for it's density
for index, row in df.iterrows():
    state_name = row['State']
    d = row['density/mi2']
    density = float(d.replace(',' , ''))
    color = cmap((density - min_density)/range_density)
    seg = map.states[state_names.index(state_name)]
    poly = Polygon(seg, facecolor=color, edgecolor=color)
    ax.add_patch(poly)
plt.show()
```

We see a color-coded density map in the following figure. I am not sure why Minnesota and Wisconsin did not match up with the data (they show no color for the density in the map). The data file looks correct and does appear to map to the image points.

 The packages used in this example would need to be installed, as they are not part of the standard set issued:

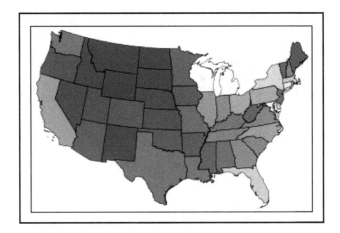

Draw a histogram of social data

There are a wide variety of social sites that produce datasets. In this example, we will gather one of the datasets and produce a histogram from the data. The specific dataset is the voting behavior on WIKI from `https://snap.stanford.edu/data/wiki-Vote.html`. Each data item shows user number N voted for user number X. So, we produce some statistics in a histogram to analyze voting behavior by:

- Gathering all of the voting that took place
- For each vote:
    - Increment a counter that says who voted
    - Increment a counter that says who was voted for
    - Massage the data so we can display it in two histograms

The coding is as follows:

```
%matplotlib inline
# import all packages being used
import matplotlib.pyplot as plt
import pandas as pd
import numpy as np
import matplotlib

# load voting data drawn from https://snap.stanford.edu/data/wiki-Vote.html
df = pd.read_table('wiki-Vote.txt', sep=r"\s+", index_col=0)

# produce standard summary info to validate
print(df.head())
print(df.describe())
```

 Python will automatically assign the first column as the index into the table, regardless of whether the index is re-used (as is this case). You can see in the `describe()` results only the `ToNodeId` column is mentioned:

	ToNodeId
FromNodeId	
30	1412
30	3352
30	5254
30	5543
30	7478

	ToNodeId
count	103689.000000
mean	3580.347018

```
std        2204.045658
min           3.000000
25%        1746.000000
50%        3260.000000
75%        5301.000000
max        8297.000000
```

Next, we produce grouped totals by the number of votes by a person and number of votes for a person. I assume there is a built-in function that would do this more nicely, but I did not find it:

```
from_counter = {}
to_counter = {}
for index, row in df.iterrows():
    ton = row['ToNodeId']
    fromn = index
    #add the from entry
    if from_counter.has_key(fromn):
        # bump entry
        from_counter[fromn] = from_counter.get(fromn) + 1
    else:
        # create entry
        from_counter[fromn] = 1
    #add the to entry
    if to_counter.has_key(ton):
        # bump entry
        to_counter[ton] = to_counter.get(ton) + 1
    else:
        # create entry
        to_counter[ton] = 1
print(from_counter)
print(to_counter)
{3: 23, 4: 29, 5: 23, 6: 302, 7: 24, 8: 182, 9: 81, 10: 86, 11: 743,...
```

We can already see some big numbers in there, like 743:

```
#extract the count values
from_counts = from_counter.values()
to_counts = to_counter.values()

print("Most votes by a user",max(from_counts))
print("Most voted for",max(to_counts))
('Most votes by a user', 893)
('Most voted for', 457)

#make histogram of number of references made by a user
plt.hist(from_counts)
plt.title("How Many Votes Made By Users")
```

```
plt.xlabel("Value")
plt.ylabel("Frequency")
plt.show()
```

We see the following plot, with the now familiar display of votes by users. I think this is one of the plainer layouts I have seen:

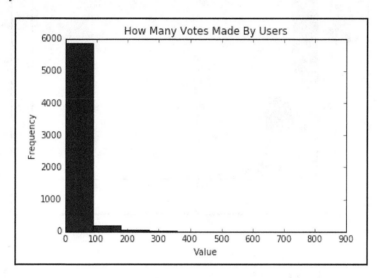

Now we make a histogram of the references made for a user with the following code:

```
#make histogram of number of references made for a user
plt.hist(to_counts)
plt.title("How Many Votes Made for User")
plt.xlabel("Value")
plt.ylabel("Frequency")
plt.show()
```

We see the votes by users plot as follows. I hadn't expected such lopsided results: only a few people vote a lot and only a few people got significant votes:

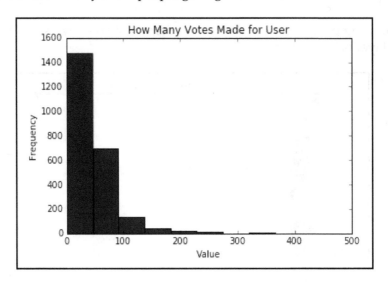

Plotting 3D data

Many of the data analysis packages (R, Python, and so on) have significant data visualization capabilities. An interesting one is to display data in three dimensions. Often, when three dimensions are used, unexpected visualizations appear.

For this example, we are using the car dataset from https://uci.edu/. It is a well-used dataset with several attributes for vehicles, for example, mpg, weight, and acceleration. What if we were to plot three of those data attributes together and see if we can recognize any apparent rules?

The coding involved is as follows:

```
%matplotlib inline
# import tools we are using
import pandas as pd
import numpy as np
from mpl_toolkits.mplot3d import Axes3D
import matplotlib.pyplot as plt
# read in the car 'table' - not a csv, so we need
# to add in the column names
column_names = ['mpg', 'cylinders', 'displacement', 'horsepower', 'weight',
'acceleration', 'year', 'origin', 'name']
```

```
df =
pd.read_table('http://archive.ics.uci.edu/ml/machine-learning-databases/aut
o-mpg/auto-mpg.data', \
                  sep=r"\s+", index_col=0, header=None, names =
column_names)
print(df.head())
      cylinders   displacement horsepower  weight   acceleration   year
origin  \
mpg
18.0            8            307.0  130.0  3504.0          12.0       70      1
15.0            8            350.0  165.0  3693.0          11.5       70      1
18.0            8            318.0  150.0  3436.0          11.0       70      1
16.0            8            304.   150.0  3433.0          12.0       70      1
17.0            8            302.   140.0  3449.0          10.5       70      1
mpg                          name
18.0   chevrolet chevelle malibu
15.0           buick skylark 320
18.0         plymouth satellite
16.0               amc rebel sst
17.0                 ford torino
```

In the following code, we plot out the data according to three axes that appear to be significant factors—weight, miles per gallon, and the number of cylinders in the engines:

```
#start out plotting (uses a subplot as that can be 3d)
fig = plt.figure()
ax = fig.add_subplot(111, projection='3d')
# pull out the 3 columns that we want
xs = []
ys = []
zs = []
for index, row in df.iterrows():
 xs.append(row['weight'])
 ys.append(index) #read_table uses first column as index
 zs.append(row['cylinders'])
# based on our data, set the extents of the axes
plt.xlim(min(xs), max(xs))
plt.ylim(min(ys), max(ys))
ax.set_zlim(min(zs), max(zs))
# standard scatter diagram (except it is 3d)
ax.scatter(xs, ys, zs)
ax.set_xlabel('Weight')
ax.set_ylabel('MPG')
ax.set_zlabel('Cylinders')
plt.show()
```

Unexpectedly, there appears to be three levels by the apparent three lines of data points, regardless of weight:

- Six cylinders with higher mpg
- A lower mpg four cylinder
- A higher mpg for four cylinder vehicles

I would have expected the weight to have a bigger effect:

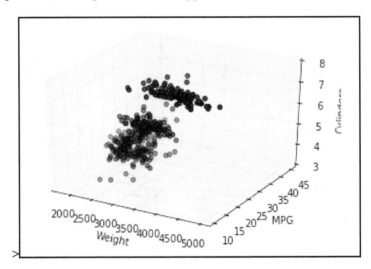

Summary

In this chapter, we used prediction models from Python and R under Jupyter. We used Matplotlib for data visualization. We used interactive plotting (under Python). And we covered several graphing techniques available in Jupyter. We created a density map with SciPy. We used histograms to visualize social data. Lastly, we generated a 3D plot under Jupyter.

In the next chapter, we will look at accessing data in different ways under Jupyter.

4

Data Mining and SQL Queries

PySpark exposes the Spark programming model to Python. Spark is a fast, general engine for large-scale data processing. We can use Python under Jupyter. So, we can use Spark in Jupyter.

Installing Spark requires the following components to be installed on your machine:

- Java JDK.
- Scala from `http://www.scala-lang.org/download/`.
- Python recommend downloading Anaconda with Python (from `http://continuum.io`).
- Spark from `https://spark.apache.org/downloads.html`.
- `winutils`: This is a command-line utility that exposes Linux commands to Windows. There are 32-bit and 64-bit versions available at:
    - 32-bit `winutils.exe` at `https://code.google.com/p/rrd-hadoop-win32/source/checkout`
    - 64-bit `winutils.exe` at `https://github.com/steveloughran/winutils/tree/master/hadoop-2.6.0/bin`

Then set environment variables that show the position of the preceding components:

- `JAVA_HOME`: The bin directory where you installed JDK
- `PYTHONPATH`: Directory where Python was installed
- `HADOOP_HOME`: Directory where `winutils` resides
- `SPARK_HOME`: Where Spark is installed

These components are readily available over the internet for a variety of operating systems. I have successfully installed these previous components in a Windows environment and a Mac environment.

Once you have these installed you should be able to run the command, `pyspark`, from a command line window and a Jupyter Notebook with Python (with access to Spark) can be used. In my installation I used the command:

```
pyspark
```

As I had installed Spark in the root with the `\spark` directory. Yes, `pyspark` is a built-in tool for use by Spark.

Special note for Windows installation

Spark (really Hadoop) needs a temporary storage location for its working set of data. Under Windows this defaults to the `\tmp\hive` location. If the directory does not exist when Spark/Hadoop starts it will create it. Unfortunately, under Windows, the installation does not have the correct tools built-in to set the access privileges to the directory.

You should be able to run `chmod` under `winutils` to set the access privileges for the `hive` directory. However, I have found that the `chmod` function does not work correctly.

A better idea has been to create the `tmp\hive` directory yourself in admin mode. And then grant full privileges to the hive directory to all users, again in admin mode.

Without this change, Hadoop fails right away. When you start `pyspark`, the output (including any errors) are displayed in the command line window. One of the errors will be insufficient access to this directory.

Using Spark to analyze data

The first thing to do in order to access Spark is to create a `SparkContext`. The `SparkContext` initializes all of Spark and sets up any access that may be needed to Hadoop, if you are using that as well.

The initial object used to be a `SQLContext`, but that has been deprecated recently in favor of `SparkContext`, which is more open-ended.

We could use a simple example to just read through a text file as follows:

```
from pyspark import SparkContext
sc = SparkContext.getOrCreate()

lines = sc.textFile("B05238_04 Spark Total Line Lengths.ipynb")
lineLengths = lines.map(lambda s: len(s))
totalLength = lineLengths.reduce(lambda a, b: a + b)
print(totalLength)
```

In this example:

- We obtain a `SparkContext`
- With the context, read in a file (the Jupyter file for this example)
- We use a Hadoop `map` function to split up the text file into different lines and gather the lengths
- We use a Hadoop `reduce` function to calculate the length of all the lines
- We display our results

Under Jupyter this looks like the following:

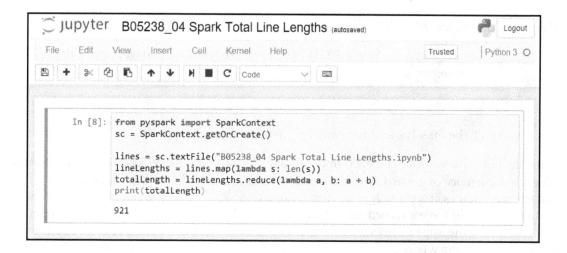

Another MapReduce example

We can use MapReduce in another example where we get the word counts from a file. A standard problem, but we use MapReduce to do most of the heavy lifting. We can use the source code for this example. We can use a script similar to this to count the word occurrences in a file:

```
import pyspark
if not 'sc' in globals():
    sc = pyspark.SparkContext()

text_file = sc.textFile("Spark File Words.ipynb")
counts = text_file.flatMap(lambda line: line.split(" ")) \
            .map(lambda word: (word, 1)) \
            .reduceByKey(lambda a, b: a + b)
for x in counts.collect():
    print x
```

We have the same preamble to the coding.

Then we load the text file into memory.

`text_file` is a Spark **RDD (Resilient Distributed Dataset)**, not a data frame.

It is assumed to be massive and the contents distributed over many handlers.

Once the file is loaded we split each line into words, and then use a `lambda` function to tick off each occurrence of a word. The code is truly creating a new record for each word occurrence, such as *at appears 1, at appears 1*. For example, if the word *at* appears twice each occurrence would have a record added like *at appears 1*. The idea is to not aggregate results yet, just record the appearances that we see. The idea is that this process could be split over multiple processors where each processor generates these low-level information bits. We are not concerned with optimizing this process at all.

Once we have all of these records we reduce/summarize the record set according to the word occurrences mentioned.

The `counts` object is also RDD in Spark. The last `for` loop runs a `collect()` against the RDD. As mentioned, this RDD could be distributed among many nodes. The `collect()` function pulls in all copies of the RDD into one location. Then we loop through each record.

When we run this in Jupyter we see something akin to this display:

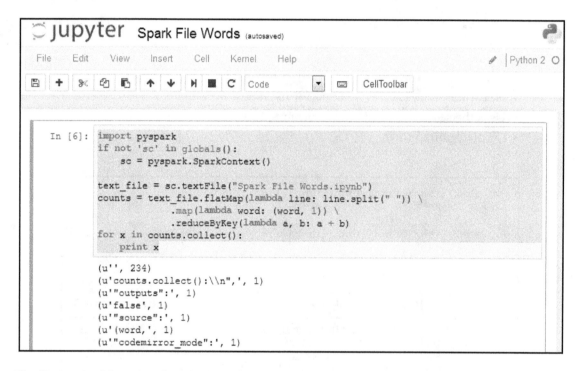

The listing is abbreviated as the list of words continues for some time.

The previous example doesn't work well with Python 3. There is a workaround when coding directly in Python, but not for Jupyter.

Using SparkSession and SQL

Spark exposes many SQL-like actions that can be taken upon a data frame. For example, we could load a data frame with product sales information in a CSV file:

```
from pyspark.sql import SparkSession
spark = SparkSession(sc)

df = spark.read.format("csv") \
        .option("header", "true") \
        .load("productsales.csv");
df.show()
```

The example:

- Starts a `SparkSession` (needed for most data access)
- Uses the session to read a CSV formatted file, that contains a header record
- Displays initial rows

```
from pyspark.sql import SparkSession
spark = SparkSession(sc)

df = spark.read.format("csv") \
        .option("header", "true") \
        .load("productsales.csv");
df.show()
```

ACTUAL	PREDICT	COUNTRY	REGION	DIVISION	PRODTYPE	PRODUCT	QUARTER	YEAR	MONTH
925	850	CANADA	EAST	EDUCATION	FURNITURE	SOFA	1	1993	12054
999	297	CANADA	EAST	EDUCATION	FURNITURE	SOFA	1	1993	12085
608	846	CANADA	EAST	EDUCATION	FURNITURE	SOFA	1	1993	12113
642	533	CANADA	EAST	EDUCATION	FURNITURE	SOFA	2	1993	12144
656	646	CANADA	EAST	EDUCATION	FURNITURE	SOFA	2	1993	12174

We have a few interesting columns in the sales data:

- Actual sales for the products by division
- Predicted sales for the products by division

If this were a bigger file, we could use SQL to determine the extent of the product list. Then the following is the Spark SQL to determine the product list:

```
df.groupBy("PRODUCT").count().show()
```

The data frame `groupBy` function works very similar to the SQL `Group By` clause. `Group By` collects the items in the dataset according to the values in the column specified. In this case the `PRODUCT` column. The `Group By` results in a dataset being established with the results. As a dataset, we can query how many rows are in each with the `count()` function.

So, the result of the `groupBy` is a count of the number of items that correspond to the grouping element. For example, we grouped the items by `CHAIR` and found 288 of them:

```
df.groupBy("PRODUCT").count().show()

+-------+-----+
|PRODUCT|count|
+-------+-----+
|  CHAIR|  288|
|    BED|  288|
|  TABLE|  288|
|   SOFA|  288|
|   DESK|  288|
+-------+-----+
```

So, we obviously do not have real product data. It is unlikely that any company has the exact same number of products in each line.

We can look into the dataset to determine how the different divisions performed in actual versus predicted sales using the `filter()` command in this example:

```
df.filter(df['ACTUAL'] > df['PREDICT']).show()
```

We pass a logical test to the `filter` command that will be operated against every row in the dataset. If the data in that row passes the test then the row is returned. Otherwise, the row is dropped from the results.

Our test is only interested in sales where the actual sales figure exceeds the predicted values.

Under Jupyter this looks as like the following:

```
df.filter(df['ACTUAL'] > df['PREDICT']).show()

+------+-------+-------+------+---------+---------+-------+-------+----+-----+
|ACTUAL|PREDICT|COUNTRY|REGION| DIVISION| PRODTYPE|PRODUCT|QUARTER|YEAR|MONTH|
+------+-------+-------+------+---------+---------+-------+-------+----+-----+
|   925|    850| CANADA|  EAST|EDUCATION|FURNITURE|   SOFA|      1|1993|12054|
|   999|    297| CANADA|  EAST|EDUCATION|FURNITURE|   SOFA|      1|1993|12085|
|   642|    533| CANADA|  EAST|EDUCATION|FURNITURE|   SOFA|      2|1993|12144|
|   656|    646| CANADA|  EAST|EDUCATION|FURNITURE|   SOFA|      2|1993|12174|
|   948|    486| CANADA|  EAST|EDUCATION|FURNITURE|   SOFA|      2|1993|12205|
```

So, we get a reduced result set. Again, this was produced by the `filter` function as a data frame and can then be called upon to `show` as any other data frame. Notice the third record from the previous display is not present as its actual sales were less than predicted. It is always a good idea to use a quick survey to make sure you have the correct results.

What if we wanted to pursue this further and determine which were the best performing areas within the company?

If this were a database table we could create another column that stored the difference between actual and predicted sales and then sort our display on that column. We can perform very similar steps in Spark.

Using a data frame we could use coding like this:

```
#register dataframe as temporary SQL table
df.createOrReplaceTempView("sales")
# pull the values by the difference calculated
sqlDF = spark.sql("SELECT *, ACTUAL-PREDICT as DIFF FROM sales ORDER BY
DIFF desc")
sqlDF.show()
```

The first statement is creating a view/data frame within the context for further manipulation. This view is lazy evaluated, will not persist unless specific steps are taken, and most importantly can be accessed as a hive view. The view is available directly from the `SparkContext`.

We then create a new data frame with the computed new column using the new sales view that we created. Under Jupyter this looks as follows:

```
#register dataframe as temp SQL table
df.createOrReplaceTempView("sales")

# pull the values by the difference calculated
sqlDF = spark.sql("SELECT *, ACTUAL-PREDICT as DIFF FROM sales ORDER BY DIFF desc")
sqlDF.show()
```

```
+------+-------+-------+------+---------+---------+-------+-------+----+-----+-----+
|ACTUAL|PREDICT|COUNTRY|REGION| DIVISION| PRODTYPE|PRODUCT|QUARTER|YEAR|MONTH| DIFF|
+------+-------+-------+------+---------+---------+-------+-------+----+-----+-----+
|   996|     50|GERMANY|  EAST|EDUCATION|   OFFICE|   DESK|      3|1993|12266|946.0|
|   972|     39| U.S.A.|  WEST|EDUCATION|   OFFICE|  TABLE|      2|1994|12570|933.0|
|   984|     65| U.S.A.|  EAST|EDUCATION|   OFFICE|   DESK|      1|1994|12419|919.0|
|   948|     50|GERMANY|  WEST|EDUCATION|FURNITURE|   SOFA|      4|1994|12723|898.0|
|   916|     18|GERMANY|  WEST| CONSUMER|FURNITURE|    BED|      4|1993|12327|898.0|
|   909|     15| CANADA|  EAST| CONSUMER|   OFFICE|   DESK|      3|1993|12235|894.0|
|   912|     23| CANADA|  EAST|EDUCATION|   OFFICE|   DESK|      1|1994|12450|889.0|
+------+-------+-------+------+---------+---------+-------+-------+----+-----+-----+
```

Again, I don't think we have realistic values as the differences are very far off from predicted values.

The data frames created are immutable, unlike database tables.

Combining datasets

So, we have seen moving a data frame into Spark for analysis. This appears to be very close to SQL tables. Under SQL it is standard practice not to reproduce items in different tables. For example, a product table might have the price and an order table would just reference the product table by product identifier, so as not to duplicate data. So, then another SQL practice is to join or combine the tables to come up with the full set of information needed. Keeping with the order analogy, we combine all of the tables involved as each table has pieces of data that are needed for the order to be complete.

How difficult would it be to create a set of tables and join them using Spark? We will use example tables of `Product`, `Order`, and `ProductOrder`:

Table	Columns
Product	Product ID, Description, Price
Order	Order ID, Order Date
ProductOrder	Order ID, Product ID, Quantity

So, an `Order` has a list of `Product`/`Quantity` values associated.

We can populate the data frames and move them into Spark:

```
from pyspark import SparkContext
from pyspark.sql import SparkSession

sc = SparkContext.getOrCreate()
spark = SparkSession(sc)

# load product set
productDF = spark.read.format("csv") \
        .option("header", "true") \
        .load("product.csv");
productDF.show()
productDF.createOrReplaceTempView("product")

# load order set
orderDF = spark.read.format("csv") \
        .option("header", "true") \
        .load("order.csv");
orderDF.show()
orderDF.createOrReplaceTempView("order")

# load order/product set
orderproductDF = spark.read.format("csv") \
        .option("header", "true") \
        .load("orderproduct.csv");
orderproductDF.show()
orderproductDF.createOrReplaceTempView("orderproduct")
```

Now, we can attempt to perform an SQL-like `JOIN` operation among them:

```
# join the tables
joinedDF = spark.sql("SELECT * " \
      "FROM orderproduct " \
      "JOIN order ON order.orderid = orderproduct.orderid " \
      "ORDER BY order.orderid")
joinedDF.show()
```

Doing all of this in Jupyter results in the display as follows:

```
from pyspark import SparkContext
from pyspark.sql import SparkSession

sc = SparkContext.getOrCreate()
spark = SparkSession(sc)
```

Our standard imports obtain a `SparkContext` and initialize a `SparkSession`. Note, the `getOrCreate` of the `SparkContext`. If you were to run this code outside of Jupyter there would be no context and a new one would be created. Under Jupyter, the startup for Spark in Jupyter initializes a context for all scripts. We can use that context at will with any Spark script, rather than have to create one ourselves.

Load our `product` table:

```
# load product set
productDF = spark.read.format("csv") \
      .option("header", "true") \
      .load("product.csv");
productDF.show()
productDF.createOrReplaceTempView("product")

+---------+-----------------+------+
|productid|      description| price|
+---------+-----------------+------+
|     1001| "Baby High Chair"| 35.00|
|     1002|  "Kitchen Table"|120.00|
|     1003|     "Phone Desk"| 20.00|
+---------+-----------------+------+
```

Load the `order` table:

```
# Load order set
orderDF = spark.read.format("csv") \
        .option("header", "true") \
        .load("order.csv");
orderDF.show()
orderDF.createOrReplaceTempView("order")


+-------+------------+
|orderid|  "orderdate"|
+-------+------------+
|   2001| '2017-07-04'|
|   2002| '2017-07-08'|
|   2003| '2017-07-09'|
+-------+------------+
```

Load the `orderproduct` table. Note that at least one of the orders has multiple products:

```
# Load order/product set
orderproductDF = spark.read.format("csv") \
        .option("header", "true") \
        .load("orderproduct.csv"); .
orderproductDF.show()
orderproductDF.createOrReplaceTempView("orderproduct")


+-------+------------+-----------+
|orderid| "productid"| "quantity"|
+-------+------------+-----------+
|   2001|        1001|          1|
|   2001|        1002|          1|
|   2002|        1003|          3|
|   2003|        1002|          1|
+-------+------------+-----------+
```

We have the `orderid` column from `order` and `orderproduct` in the result set. We could be more selective in our query and specify the exact columns we want to be returned:

```
# join the tables
joinedDF = spark.sql("SELECT * " \
                "FROM orderproduct " \
                "JOIN order ON order.orderid = orderproduct.orderid " \
                "ORDER BY order.orderid")
joinedDF.show()

+-------+-----------+-----------+-------+-----------+
|orderid| "productid"| "quantity"|orderid|  "orderdate"|
+-------+-----------+-----------+-------+-----------+
|   2001|       1001|          1|   2001| '2017-07-04'|
|   2001|       1002|          1|   2001| '2017-07-04'|
|   2002|       1003|          3|   2002| '2017-07-08'|
|   2003|       1002|          1|   2003| '2017-07-09'|
+-------+-----------+-----------+-------+-----------+
```

 I had tried to use the Spark `join()` command with no luck.

The documentation and examples I found on the internet are old, sparse, and incorrect.

Using the command also presented the persistent error of a task not returning results in time. From the underlying Hadoop, I expect that processing tasks are normally broken up into separate tasks. I assume that Spark is breaking up functions into separate threads for completion similarly. It is not clear why such minor tasks are not completing as I was not asking it to perform anything extraordinary.

Loading JSON into Spark

Spark can also access JSON data for manipulation. Here we have an example that:

- Loads a JSON file into a Spark data frame
- Examines the contents of the data frame and displays the apparent schema
- Like the other preceding data frames, moves the data frame into the context for direct access by the Spark session
- Shows an example of accessing the data frame in the Spark context

The listing is as follows:

Our standard includes for Spark:

```
from pyspark import SparkContext
from pyspark.sql import SparkSession
sc = SparkContext.getOrCreate()
spark = SparkSession(sc)
```

Read in the JSON and display what we found:

```
#using some data from file from
https://gist.github.com/marktyers/678711152b8dd33f6346
df = spark.read.json("people.json")
df.show()
```

```
from pyspark import SparkContext
from pyspark.sql import SparkSession

sc = SparkContext.getOrCreate()
spark = SparkSession(sc)

#using some data from file from https://gist.github.com/marktyers/678711152b8dd33f6346
df = spark.read.json("people.json")
df.show()
+----+----+--------------------+---------------+
| age|born|                fame|           name|
+----+----+--------------------+---------------+
|null|null|                null|        Michael|
|  30|null|                null|           Andy|
|  19|null|                null|         Justin|
|null|1955|co-founder of App...|     Steve Jobs|
|null|1955|                null|Tim Berners-Lee|
|null|1815|                null|   George Boole|
+----+----+--------------------+---------------+
```

I had a difficult time getting a standard JSON to load into Spark. Spark appears to expect one record of data per list of the JSON file versus most JSON I have seen pretty much formats the record layouts with indentation and the like.

 Notice the use of null values where an attribute was not specified in an instance.

Display the interpreted schema for the data:

```
df.printSchema()
```

```
df.printSchema()

root
 |-- age: long (nullable = true)
 |-- born: long (nullable = true)
 |-- fame: string (nullable = true)
 |-- name: string (nullable = true)
```

The default for all columns is `nullable`. You can change an attribute of a column, but you cannot change the value of a column as the data values are immutable.

Move the data frame into the context and access it from there:

```
df.registerTempTable("people")
spark.sql("select name from people").show()
```

```
df.registerTempTable("people")
spark.sql("select name from people").show()

+---------------+
|           name|
+---------------+
|        Michael|
|           Andy|
|         Justin|
|     Steve Jobs|
|Tim Berners-Lee|
|   George Boole|
+---------------+
```

At this point, the `people` table works like any other temporary SQL table in Spark.

Using Spark pivot

The `pivot()` function allows you to translate rows into columns while performing aggregation on some of the columns. If you think about it you are physically adjusting the axes of a table about a pivot point.

I thought of an easy example to show how this all works. I think it is one of those features that once you see it in action you realize the number of areas that you could apply it.

In our example, we have some raw price points for stocks and we want to convert that table about a pivot to produce average prices per year per stock.

The code in our example is:

```
from pyspark import SparkContext
from pyspark.sql import SparkSession
from pyspark.sql import functions as func

sc = SparkContext.getOrCreate()
spark = SparkSession(sc)

# load product set
pivotDF = spark.read.format("csv") \
        .option("header", "true") \
        .load("pivot.csv");
pivotDF.show()
pivotDF.createOrReplaceTempView("pivot")

# pivot data per the year to get average prices per stock per year
pivotDF \
    .groupBy("stock") \
    .pivot("year",[2012,2013]) \
    .agg(func.avg("price")) \
    .show()
```

This looks as follows in Jupyter:

```
from pyspark import SparkContext
from pyspark.sql import SparkSession
from pyspark.sql import functions as func

sc = SparkContext.getOrCreate()
spark = SparkSession(sc)
```

All the standard includes what we need for Spark to initialize the `SparkContext` and the `SparkSession`:

```
# Load product set
pivotDF = spark.read.format("csv") \
         .option("header", "true") \
         .load("pivot.csv");
pivotDF.show()
pivotDF.createOrReplaceTempView("pivot")

+-----+----+-----+
|stock|year|price|
+-----+----+-----+
|  IBM|2012|  100|
| MSFT|2012|   45|
|  IBM|2012|  105|
|  IBM|2013|  144|
| MSFT|2013|   47|
+-----+----+-----+
```

We load the stock price information from a CSV file. It is important that at least one of the stocks have more than one price for the same year:

```
# pivot data per the year to get average prices per stock per year
pivotDF \
    .groupBy("stock") \
    .pivot("year",[2012,2013]) \
    .agg(func.avg("price")) \
    .show()

+-----+-----+-----+
|stock| 2012| 2013|
+-----+-----+-----+
|  IBM|102.5|144.0|
| MSFT| 45.0| 47.0|
+-----+-----+-----+
```

We are grouping the information by stock symbol. The pivot is on the year that has two values, 2012 and 2013, in our dataset. We are computing an average price for each year.

Summary

In this chapter, we got familiar with obtaining a `SparkContext`. We saw examples of using Hadoop MapReduce. We used SQL with Spark data. We combined data frames and operated on the resulting set. We imported JSON data and manipulated it with Spark. Lastly, we looked at using a pivot to gather information about a data frame.

In the next chapter, we will look at using R programming under Jupyter.

5
R with Jupyter

In this chapter we will be using R coding within Jupyter. I think R is one of the primary languages expected to be used within Jupyter. The full extent of the language is available to Jupyter users.

How to set up R for Jupyter

In the past, it was necessary to install the separate components of Jupyter, Python, and so on to have a working system. With Continuum Analytics, the process of installing Jupyter and adding the R engine to the solution set for Jupyter is easy and works on both Windows and Mac.

Assuming you have installed conda already, we have one command to add support for R programming to Jupyter:

```
conda install -c r r-essentials
```

 At this point, when you start Jupyter, one of the kernels listed will now be **R**.

R data analysis of the 2016 US election demographics

To get a flavor of the resources available to R developers, we can look at the 2016 election data. In this case, I am drawing from Wikipedia (`https://en.wikipedia.org/wiki/United_States_presidential_election,_2016`), specifically the table named 2016 presidential vote by demographic subgroup. We have the following coding below.

Define a helper function so we can print out values easily. The new `printf` function takes any arguments passed (`...`) and passes them along to `sprintf`:

```
printf <- function(...)print(sprintf(...))
```

I have stored the separate demographic statistics into different **TSV (tab-separated value)** files, which can be read in using the following coding. For each table, we use the `read.csv` function and specify the field separator as a tab instead of the default comma. We then use the `head` function to display information about the data frame that was loaded:

```
age <- read.csv("Documents/B05238_05_age.tsv", sep="\t")
head(age)

education <- read.csv("Documents/B05238_05_education.tsv", sep="\t")
head(education)

gender <- read.csv("Documents/B05238_05_gender.tsv", sep="\t")
head(gender)

ideology <- read.csv("Documents/B05238_05_ideology.tsv", sep="\t")
head(ideology)

income <- read.csv("Documents/B05238_05_income.tsv", sep="\t")
head(income)

orientation <- read.csv("Documents/B05238_05_orientation.tsv", sep="\t")
head(orientation)

party <- read.csv("Documents/B05238_05_party.tsv", sep="\t")
head(party)

race <- read.csv("Documents/B05238_05_race.tsv", sep="\t")
head(race)

region <- read.csv("Documents/B05238_05_region.tsv", sep="\t")
head(region)
```

```
religion <- read.csv("Documents/B05238_05_religion.tsv", sep="\t")
head(religion)
```

Across the top is a display of the columns. Every row displays the values for those columns in that row. Each of these `read` operations results in a display as follows:

In [212]:
```
printf <- function(...)print(sprintf(...))
```

In [213]:
```
age <- read.csv("Documents/B05238_05_age.tsv", sep="\t")
head(age)
```

age	Clinton	Trump
18-24 years old	56	35
25-29 years old	53	39
30-39 years old	51	40
40-49 years old	46	50
50-64 years old	44	53
65 and older	45	53

Now, we can find the dominant characteristics of each turnout:

```
printf("Most Clinton voters from %s",age[which.max(age$Clinton),'age'])
printf("Most Clinton voters from
%s",education[which.max(education$Clinton),'education'])
printf("Most Clinton voters from
%s",gender[which.max(gender$Clinton),'gender'])
printf("Most Clinton voters from
%s",ideology[which.max(ideology$Clinton),'ideology'])
printf("Most Clinton voters from
%s",income[which.max(income$Clinton),'income'])
printf("Most Clinton voters from
%s",orientation[which.max(orientation$Clinton),'orientation'])
printf("Most Clinton voters from
%s",party[which.max(party$Clinton),'party'])
printf("Most Clinton voters from %s",race[which.max(race$Clinton),'race'])
printf("Most Clinton voters from
%s",region[which.max(region$Clinton),'region'])
printf("Most Clinton voters from
%s",religion[which.max(religion$Clinton),'religion'])

printf("Most Trump voters from %s",age[which.max(age$Trump),'age'])
printf("Most Trump voters from
%s",education[which.max(education$Trump),'education'])
printf("Most Trump voters from
```

```
%s",gender[which.max(gender$Trump),'gender'])
printf("Most Trump voters from
%s",ideology[which.max(ideology$Trump),'ideology'])
printf("Most Trump voters from
%s",income[which.max(income$Trump),'income'])
printf("Most Trump voters from
%s",orientation[which.max(orientation$Trump),'orientation'])
printf("Most Trump voters from %s",party[which.max(party$Trump),'party'])
printf("Most Trump voters from %s",race[which.max(race$Trump),'race'])
printf("Most Trump voters from
%s",region[which.max(region$Trump),'region'])
printf("Most Trump voters from
%s",religion[which.max(religion$Trump),'religion'])
```

The results are as follows for Clinton:

```
[1] "Most Clinton voters from 18-24 years old"
[1] "Most Clinton voters from Postgraduate education"
[1] "Most Clinton voters from Women"
[1] "Most Clinton voters from Liberals"
[1] "Most Clinton voters from Under $30,000"
[1] "Most Clinton voters from LGBT"
[1] "Most Clinton voters from Democrats"
[1] "Most Clinton voters from Black"
[1] "Most Clinton voters from Northeast"
[1] "Most Clinton voters from Jewish"
```

The results for Trump are as follows:

```
[1] "Most Trump voters from 50-64 years old"
[1] "Most Trump voters from Some college education"
[1] "Most Trump voters from Men"
[1] "Most Trump voters from Conservatives"
[1] "Most Trump voters from $50,000-99,999"
[1] "Most Trump voters from Heterosexual"
[1] "Most Trump voters from Republicans"
[1] "Most Trump voters from White"
[1] "Most Trump voters from South"
[1] "Most Trump voters from Mormon"
```

It's interesting that there was no overlap between the majority groups supporting the two candidates. I think the parties targeted different groups on purpose so as not to overlap. There must be a guideline for spending money, by advertising to known, interested groups and not contend for population segments that are ambiguous.

Analyzing 2016 voter registration and voting

Similarly, we can look at voter registration versus actual voting (using census data from https://www.census.gov/data/tables/time-series/demo/voting-and-registration/p20-580.html).

First, we load our dataset and display head information to visually check for accurate loading:

```
df <- read.csv("Documents/B05238_05_registration.csv")
summary(df)
```

```
df <- read.csv("Documents/B05238_05_registration.csv")
summary(df)

       ï..state      population        citizens        registered
 ALABAMA    : 1   Min.   :  436   Min.   :  427   Min.   :  304.0
 ALASKA     : 1   1st Qu.: 1316   1st Qu.: 1243   1st Qu.:  871.5
 ARIZONA    : 1   Median : 3348   Median : 3246   Median : 2253.0
 ARKANSAS   : 1   Mean   : 4814   Mean   : 4393   Mean   : 3090.1
 CALIFORNIA : 1   3rd Qu.: 5483   3rd Qu.: 5036   3rd Qu.: 3783.0
 COLORADO   : 1   Max.   :29894   Max.   :24890   Max.   :16096.0
 (Other)    :45
     voted
 Min.   :  277.0
 1st Qu.:  738.5
 Median : 1942.0
 Mean   : 2696.8
 3rd Qu.: 3348.5
 Max.   :14416.0
```

So, we have some registration and voting information by state. Use R to automatically plot all the data in *x* and *y* format using the `plot` command:

```
plot(df)
```

We are specifically looking at the relationship between registering to vote and actually voting. We can see in the following graphic that most of the data is highly correlated (as evidenced by the 45 degree angles of most of the relationships):

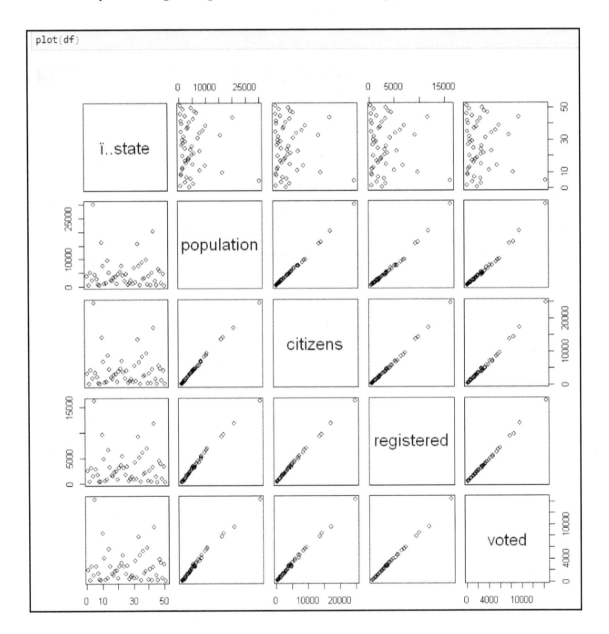

We can produce somewhat similar results using Python, but the graphic display is not even close.

Import all of the packages we are using for the example:

```
from numpy import corrcoef, sum, log, arange
from numpy.random import rand
from pylab import pcolor, show, colorbar, xticks, yticks
import pandas as pd
import matplotlib
from matplotlib import pyplot as plt
```

Reading a CSV file in Python is very similar. We call upon pandas to read in the file:

```
df
```

pandas will throw an error if there is string data in the data frame, so just delete the column (with state names):

```
del df['state'] #pandas do not deal well with strings
```

One approximate Python function is the `corr()` function, which prints out the numeric values for all of the cross-correlations among the items in the data frame. It is up to you to scan through the data, looking for correlation values close to `1.0`:

```
#print cross-correlation matrix
print(df.corr())
```

Similarly, we have the `corrcoef()` function, which provides color intensity to similarly correlated items within the data frame. I did not find a way to label the correlated items:

```
#graph same
fig = plt.gcf()
fig.set_size_inches(10, 10)
# plotting the correlation matrix
R = corrcoef(df)
pcolor(R)
colorbar()
yticks(arange(0.5,10.5),range(0,10))
xticks(arange(0.5,10.5),range(0,10))
show()
```

	population	citizens	registered	voted
population	1.000000	0.998293	0.993263	0.992711
citizens	0.998293	1.000000	0.997778	0.996752
registered	0.993263	0.997778	1.000000	0.998946
voted	0.992711	0.996752	0.998946	1.000000

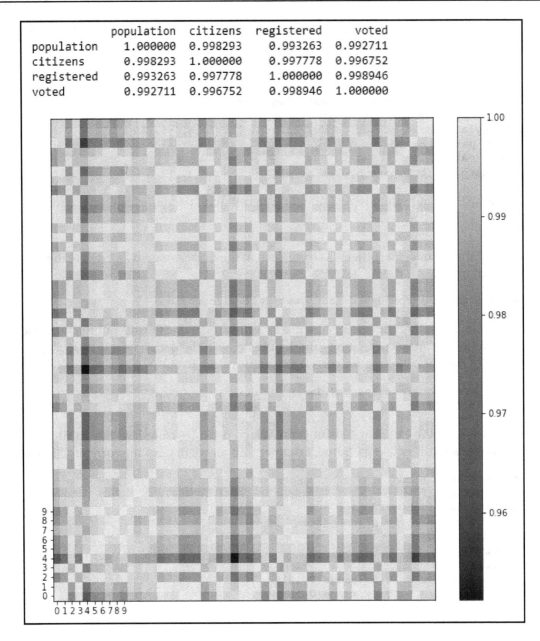

We want to see the actual numeric value of the correlation between registration and voting. We can do that by calling the `cor` function to pass in the two data points of interest, as in:

```
cor(df$voted, df$registered)
0.998946393424037
```

The actual correlation value may be different from one machine class to another. This would have a trickling affect to follow-on values as well.

With a correlation of 99 percent, we are almost perfect.

We can use the data points to arrive at a regression line using the `lm` function, where we are stating *lm(y ~ (predicted by) x)*:

```
fit <- lm(df$voted ~ df$registered)
fit
Call:
lm(formula = df$voted ~ df$registered)

Coefficients:
  (Intercept)   df$registered
    -4.1690        0.8741
```

From this output, given a registered number, we multiply it by 87 percent and subtract 4 to get the number of actual voters. Again, the data is correlated.

We can display the characteristics of the regression line by calling the `plot` function and passing in the `fit` object (the `par` function is used to lay out the output—in this case a 2x2 matrix-like display of the four graphics):

```
par(mfrow=c(2,2))
plot(fit)
```

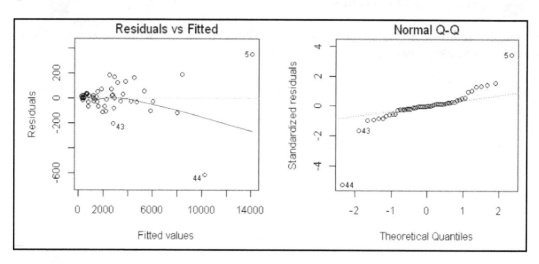

Then, in the second part of the 2x2 display, we have these two graphics:

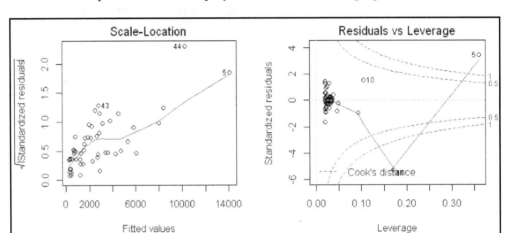

From the preceding plots we can see the following:

- The residual values are close to zero until we get to very large numbers
- The theoretical quantiles versus standardized residuals line up very well for most of the range
- The fitted values versus standardized residuals are not as close as I would have expected
- The standardized residuals versus leverage show the same tight configuration among most of the values.

Overall, we still have a very good model for the data. We can see what the residuals look like for the regression calling the `residuals` function, as follows:

```
residuals(fit)
```

1	-108.710711945375
2	-0.745053216693167
3	24.2451262681648
4	-27.4647456908974
5	351.27268798623
6	182.508662245854
7	49.1983275426326
8	-4.49900615764172
9	17.0631244396007
10	187.680924363831

```
... (for all 50 states)
```

The residual values are bigger than I expected for such highly correlated data. I had expected to see very small numbers as opposed to values in the hundreds.

As always, let's display a summary of the model that we arrived at:

```
summary(fit)
Call:
lm(formula = df$voted ~ df$registered)

Residuals:
    Min      1Q  Median      3Q     Max
-617.33  -29.69    0.83   30.70  351.27

Coefficients:
                Estimate Std. Error t value Pr(>|t|)
(Intercept)    -4.169018  25.201730  -0.165    0.869
df$registered   0.874062   0.005736 152.370   <2e-16 ***
---
Signif. codes:  0 '***' 0.001 '**' 0.01 '*' 0.05 '.' 0.1 ' ' 1

Residual standard error: 127.9 on 49 degrees of freedom
Multiple R-squared:  0.9979,  Adjusted R-squared:  0.9979
F-statistic: 2.322e+04 on 1 and 49 DF,  p-value: < 2.2e-16
```

You may see different results based on the machine class that you are running your script on.

There are many data points associated with the model in this display:

- Again, residuals are showing quite a range
- Coefficients are as we saw them earlier, but the standard error is high for the intercept
- R squared of close to 1 is expected
- *p* value minimal is expected

We can also use Python to arrive at a linear regression model using:

```
import numpy as np
import statsmodels.formula.api as sm

model = sm.ols(formula='voted ~ registered', data=df)
fitted = model.fit()
print (fitted.summary())
```

We see the regression results in standard fashion as follows:

```
                            OLS Regression Results
==============================================================================
Dep. Variable:                  voted   R-squared:                       0.998
Model:                            OLS   Adj. R-squared:                  0.998
Method:                 Least Squares   F-statistic:                 2.322e+04
Date:                Wed, 26 Jul 2017   Prob (F-statistic):           3.02e-67
Time:                        23:55:31   Log-Likelihood:                -318.77
No. Observations:                  51   AIC:                             641.5
Df Residuals:                      49   BIC:                             645.4
Df Model:                           1
Covariance Type:            nonrobust
==============================================================================
                 coef    std err          t      P>|t|      [0.025      0.975]
------------------------------------------------------------------------------
Intercept     -4.1690     25.202     -0.165      0.869     -54.814      46.476
registered     0.8741      0.006    152.370      0.000       0.863       0.886
==============================================================================
Omnibus:                       41.045   Durbin-Watson:                   1.608
Prob(Omnibus):                  0.000   Jarque-Bera (JB):              252.235
Skew:                          -1.800   Prob(JB):                     1.69e-55
Kurtosis:                      13.283   Cond. No.                      6.18e+03
==============================================================================

Warnings:
[1] Standard Errors assume that the covariance matrix of the errors is correctly specified.
[2] The condition number is large, 6.18e+03. This might indicate that there are
strong multicollinearity or other numerical problems.
```

The warnings infer some issues with the data:

- We are using the covariance matrix directly, so it is unclear how we would specify this otherwise
- I imagine there is strong multicollinearity as the data only has the two items

We can also plot the actual versus fitted values in Python using a script:

```
plt.plot(df['voted'], df['registered'], 'ro')
plt.plot(df['voted'], fitted.fittedvalues, 'b')
plt.legend(['Data', 'Fitted model'])
plt.xlabel('Voted')
plt.ylabel('Registered')
plt.title('Voted vs Registered')
plt.show()
```

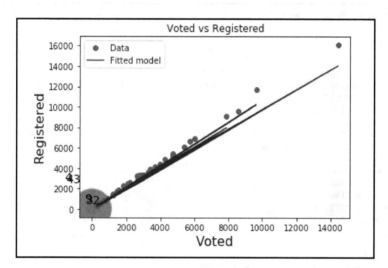

I think I like this version of the graph from Python better than the display from R. The added intensity circle on the bottom left is confusing.

Analyzing changes in college admissions

We can look at trends in college admissions acceptance rates over the last few years. For this analysis, I am using the data on `https://www.ivywise.com/ivywise-knowledgebase/admission-statistics`.

First, we read in our dataset and show the summary points, from head to validate:

```
df <- read.csv("Documents/acceptance-rates.csv")
summary(df)
head(df)
```

We see the summary data for school acceptance rates as follows:

```
df <- read.csv("Documents/acceptance-rates.csv")
summary(df)
head(df)

         ï..School        X2017            X2016            X2015
 Amherst College   : 1   Min.   :0.0500   Min.   :0.0500   Min.   :0.0500
 Boston College    : 1   1st Qu.:0.0800   1st Qu.:0.0900   1st Qu.:0.0900
 Brown University  : 1   Median :0.1000   Median :0.1300   Median :0.1300
 Columbia University: 1  Mean   :0.1444   Mean   :0.1493   Mean   :0.1534
 Cornell University : 1  3rd Qu.:0.1800   3rd Qu.:0.1700   3rd Qu.:0.1800
 Dartmouth College : 1   Max.   :0.4100   Max.   :0.4000   Max.   :0.4600
 (Other)           :23   NA's   :2
      X2007
 Min.   :0.1000
 1st Qu.:0.1600
 Median :0.2100
 Mean   :0.2279
 3rd Qu.:0.2700
 Max.   :0.5000
```

ï..School	X2017	X2016	X2015	X2007
Amherst College	NA	0.14	0.14	0.18
Boston College	0.32	0.32	0.28	0.27
Brown University	0.08	0.09	0.09	0.15
Columbia University	0.06	0.06	0.06	0.12
Cornell University	0.13	0.14	0.15	0.21
Dartmouth College	0.10	0.11	0.10	0.18

It's interesting to note that the acceptance rate varies so widely, from a low of 5 percent to a high of 41 percent in 2017.

Let us look at the data plots, again, to validate that the data points are correct:

```
plot(df)
```

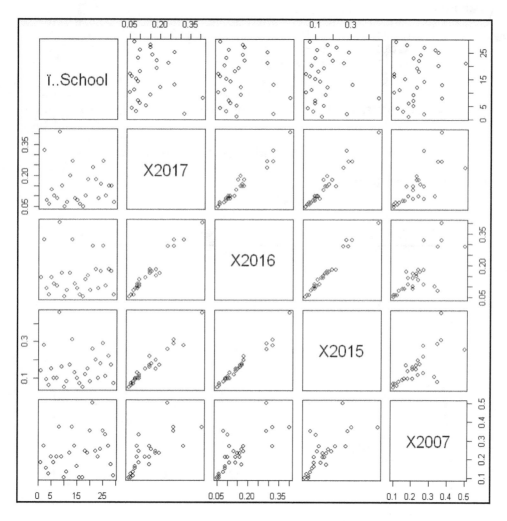

From the correlation graphics shown, it does not look like we can use the data points from 2007. The graphs show a big divergence between 2007 and the other years, whereas the other three have good correlations.

So, we have 3 consecutive years of data from 25 major US universities. We can convert the data into a time series using a few steps.

First, we create a vector of the average acceptance rates for these colleges over the years 2015-2017. We use the mean function to determine the average across all colleges in our data frame. We have some NA values in our data frame, so we need to tell the mean function to ignore those values (na.rm=TRUE):

```
myvector <- c(mean(df[["X2015"]],na.rm=TRUE),
    mean(df[["X2016"]],na.rm=TRUE),
    mean(df[["X2017"]],na.rm=TRUE))
```

Next, we convert the vector points into a time series. A time series is passed in the vector to use the start and end points, and the frequency of the data points. In our case, the frequency is yearly, so frequency = 1:

```
ts <- ts(myvector, start=c(2015), end=c(2017), frequency=1)
```

Then plot the time series to get a good visual:

```
plot(ts)
```

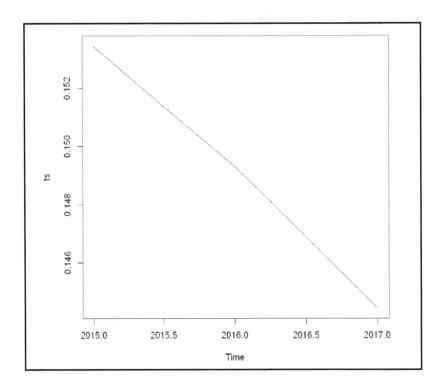

So, the clear trend is to drop acceptance rates across the board, as we see the initial acceptance rate at .15 dropping steadily to .14 in 2017.

The data looks very good and well-fitting, as data points are lining up in clean lines. We can use this time series to predict the next few years. There are versions of the Holt-Winters algorithm that can predict based on level data, level data plus a trend component, and level data plus a trend component plus a seasonality component. We have a trend, but no seasonality:

```
# double exponential - models level and trend
fit <- HoltWinters(ts, gamma=FALSE)
fit
Holt-Winters exponential smoothing with trend and without seasonal
component.

Call:
HoltWinters(x = ts, gamma = FALSE)

Smoothing parameters:
 alpha: 0.3
 beta : 0.1
 gamma: FALSE

Coefficients:
        [,1]
a  0.14495402
b -0.00415977
```

Our coefficients for the exponential smoothing of one-seventh and close to zero mean we aren't aggressively dropping acceptance rates, but they are dropping.

Now that we have a good time series model of the existing data, we can produce a forecast of the next three years and plot it:

```
install.packages("forecast", repos="http://cran.us.r-project.org")
library(forecast)
forecast(fit, 3)
plot(forecast(fit, 3))
```

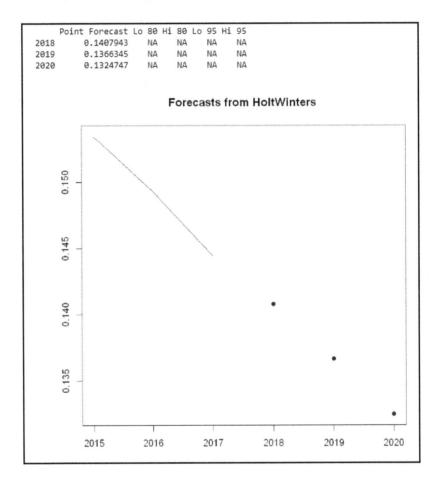

The trend is clearly negative, but as mentioned earlier, it is not a dramatic drop-about half a percent a year. We can also look at similar coding from Python that could be used as follows. Import all of the Python packages we will be using:

```
import pandas as pd
import numpy as np
import matplotlib.pylab as plt
```

```
%matplotlib inline
from matplotlib.pylab import rcParams
rcParams['figure.figsize'] = 15, 6
```

Read in the college acceptance to a data frame:

```
data = pd.read_csv('Documents/acceptance-rates.csv')
print (data.head())
               School 2017  2016  2015  2007
0     Amherst College  NaN  0.14  0.14  0.18
1     Boston College   0.32 0.32  0.28  0.27
2    Brown University  0.08 0.09  0.09  0.15
3  Columbia University 0.06 0.06  0.06  0.12
4   Cornell University 0.13 0.14  0.15  0.21
```

Remove the School column as Python cannot calculate from strings:

```
del data['School']
print (data.head())
    2017  2016  2015  2007
0   NaN   0.14  0.14  0.18
1   0.32  0.32  0.28  0.27
2   0.08  0.09  0.09  0.15
3   0.06  0.06  0.06  0.12
4   0.13  0.14  0.15  0.21
```

Convert the data to sets by year:

```
data = data.transpose()
print (data.head())
```

We see the dataset transposed to our desired shape as follows:

```
         0     1     2     3     4     5     6     7     8     9    ...     19   \
2017   NaN  0.32  0.08  0.06  0.13  0.10  0.09  0.41  0.15  0.05   ...    NaN
2016  0.14  0.32  0.09  0.06  0.14  0.11  0.10  0.40  0.16  0.05   ...   0.08
2015  0.14  0.28  0.09  0.06  0.15  0.10  0.10  0.46  0.16  0.05   ...   0.08
2007  0.18  0.27  0.15  0.12  0.21  0.18  0.21  0.37  0.21  0.10   ...   0.35

        20    21    22    23    24    25    26    27    28
2017  0.24  0.18  0.09  0.16  0.27  0.10  0.15  0.15  0.07
2016  0.29  0.18  0.09  0.17  0.29  0.10  0.18  0.17  0.06
2015  0.26  0.20  0.10  0.18  0.29  0.11  0.22  0.17  0.07
2007  0.50  0.24  0.21  0.25  0.35  0.33  0.27  0.17  0.11

[4 rows x 29 columns]
```

See what the data looks like:

```
plt.plot(data);
```

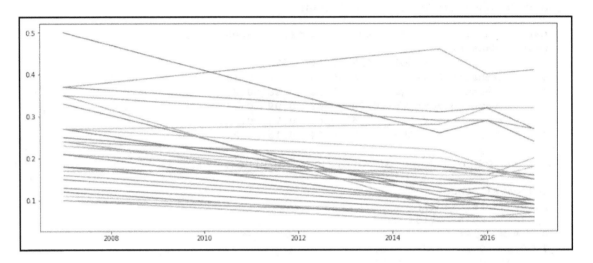

We see the same slight downtrend for acceptance.

Using Holt-Winters forecasting in Python was problematic as it required transforming the data further. Overall, it is much more complicated to do the same processing that was straightforward in R in the preceding section.

Predicting airplane arrival time

R has built-in functionality for splitting up a data frame between training and testing sets, building a model based on the training set, predicting results using the model and the testing set, and then visualizing how well the model is working.

For this example, I am using airline arrival and departure times versus scheduled arrival and departure times from http://stat-computing.org/dataexpo/2009/the-data.html for 2008. The dataset is distributed as a .bz2 file that unpacks into a CSV file. I like this dataset, as the initial row count is over 7 million and it all works nicely in Jupyter.

We first read in the airplane data and display a summary. There are additional columns in the dataset that we are not using:

```
df <- read.csv("Documents/2008-airplane.csv")
summary(df)
...
```

```
 CRSElapsedTime       AirTime            ArrDelay           DepDelay
 Min.   :-141.0    Min.   :   0      Min.   :-519.00    Min.   :-534.00
 1st Qu.:  80.0    1st Qu.:  55      1st Qu.: -10.00    1st Qu.:  -4.00
 Median : 110.0    Median :  86      Median :  -2.00    Median :  -1.00
 Mean   : 128.9    Mean   : 104      Mean   :   8.17    Mean   :   9.97
 3rd Qu.: 159.0    3rd Qu.: 132      3rd Qu.:  12.00    3rd Qu.:   8.00
 Max.   :1435.0    Max.   :1350      Max.   :2461.00    Max.   :2467.00
 NA's   :844       NA's   :154699    NA's   :154699     NA's   :136246
      Origin             Dest              Distance           TaxiIn
 ATL    : 414513   ATL    : 414521   Min.   :  11.0     Min.   :  0.00
 ORD    : 350380   ORD    : 350452   1st Qu.: 325.0     1st Qu.:  4.00
 DFW    : 281281   DFW    : 281401   Median : 581.0     Median :  6.00
 DEN    : 241443   DEN    : 241470   Mean   : 726.4     Mean   :  6.86
 LAX    : 215608   LAX    : 215685   3rd Qu.: 954.0     3rd Qu.:  8.00
 PHX    : 199408   PHX    : 199416   Max.   :4962.0     Max.   :308.00
 (Other):5307095   (Other):5306783                      NA's   :151649
     TaxiOut           Cancelled         CancellationCode    Diverted
 Min.   :  0.00    Min.   :0.00000    :6872294         Min.   :0.000000
 1st Qu.: 10.00    1st Qu.:0.00000   A:  54330         1st Qu.:0.000000
 Median : 14.00    Median :0.00000   B:  54904         Median :0.000000
 Mean   : 16.45    Mean   :0.01961   C:  28188         Mean   :0.002463
 3rd Qu.: 19.00    3rd Qu.:0.00000   D:     12         3rd Qu.:0.000000
 Max.   :429.00    Max.   :1.00000                     Max.   :1.000000
 NA's   :137058
   CarrierDelay       WeatherDelay        NASDelay          SecurityDelay
 Min.   :   0      Min.   :   0      Min.   :   0       Min.   :  0
 1st Qu.:   0      1st Qu.:   0      1st Qu.:   0       1st Qu.:  0
 Median :   0      Median :   0      Median :   6       Median :  0
 Mean   :  16      Mean   :   3      Mean   :  17       Mean   :  0
 3rd Qu.:  16      3rd Qu.:   0      3rd Qu.:  21       3rd Qu.:  0
 Max.   :2436      Max.   :1352      Max.   :1357       Max.   :392
 NA's   :5484993   NA's   :5484993   NA's   :5484993    NA's   :5484993
 LateAircraftDelay
 Min.   :   0
 1st Qu.:   0
 Median :   0
 Mean   :  21
 3rd Qu.:  26
 Max.   :1316
 NA's   :5484993
```

Many of the data points have NA values. We need to remove these in order to build an accurate model:

```
# eliminate rows with NA values
df <- na.omit(df)
```

Let's create our partitions:

```
# for partitioning to work data has to be ordered
times <- df[order(df$ArrTime),]
nrow(times)
1524735

# partition data - 75% training
library(caret)
set.seed(1337)
trainingIndices <- createDataPartition(df$ArrTime,p=0.75,list=FALSE)
trainingSet <- df[trainingIndices,]
testingSet <- df[-trainingIndices,]
nrow(trainingSet)
nrow(testingSet)
1143553
381182
```

Let's build our model of the arrival time (ArrTime) based on the fields:

- CRSArrTime: Scheduled arrival time
- ArrDelay: Arrival delay
- DepDelay: Departure delay
- Diverted: Whether the plane used a diverted route
- CarrierDelay: Delay by the carrier systems
- WeatherDelay: Delay due to weather
- NASDelay: Delay due to NAS
- SecurityDelay: Delay due to security
- LateAircraftDelay: Plane arrived late due to other delay

```
model <- lm(ArrTime ~ CRSArrTime + ArrDelay + DepDelay + Diverted +
        CarrierDelay + WeatherDelay + NASDelay + SecurityDelay + LateAircraftDelay,
        data=trainingSet)
summary(model)
```

```
Call:
lm(formula = ArrTime ~ CRSArrTime + ArrDelay + DepDelay + Diverted +
    CarrierDelay + WeatherDelay + NASDelay + SecurityDelay +
    LateAircraftDelay, data = trainingSet)

Residuals:
   Min     1Q  Median     3Q     Max
-2139.0  -62.2   91.9  215.6  3739.7

Coefficients: (2 not defined because of singularities)
                   Estimate Std. Error t value Pr(>|t|)
(Intercept)       5.318e+02  1.654e+00 321.584  < 2e-16 ***
CRSArrTime        6.814e-01  9.567e-04 712.243  < 2e-16 ***
ArrDelay         -1.806e+00  2.877e-02 -62.763  < 2e-16 ***
DepDelay          3.065e-01  2.492e-02  12.299  < 2e-16 ***
Diverted                 NA         NA      NA       NA
CarrierDelay      8.872e-01  1.505e-02  58.962  < 2e-16 ***
WeatherDelay      6.033e-01  2.528e-02  23.867  < 2e-16 ***
NASDelay          1.690e+00  1.945e-02  86.930  < 2e-16 ***
SecurityDelay     7.563e-01  2.369e-01   3.192  0.00141 **
LateAircraftDelay        NA         NA      NA       NA
---
Signif. codes:  0 '***' 0.001 '**' 0.01 '*' 0.05 '.' 0.1 ' ' 1

Residual standard error: 473.4 on 1143545 degrees of freedom
Multiple R-squared:  0.3134,    Adjusted R-squared:  0.3134
F-statistic: 7.458e+04 on 7 and 1143545 DF,  p-value: < 2.2e-16
```

Two of the data items are just flags (0/1), unfortunately. The greatest predictor appears to be the scheduled arrival time. The other various delay factors have small effects. I think it just feels as if it's taking an extra 20 minutes for a security check or the like; it's a big deal when you are traveling.

Now that we have a model, let's use the testing set to make predictions:

```
predicted <- predict(model, newdata=testingSet)
summary(predicted)
summary(testingSet$ArrTime)
   Min. 1st Qu.  Median    Mean 3rd Qu.    Max.
   -941    1360    1629    1590    1843    2217
   Min. 1st Qu.  Median    Mean 3rd Qu.    Max.
      1    1249    1711    1590    2034    2400
```

Plot out the predicted versus actual data to get a sense of the model's accuracy:

```
plot(predicted,testingSet$ArrTime)
```

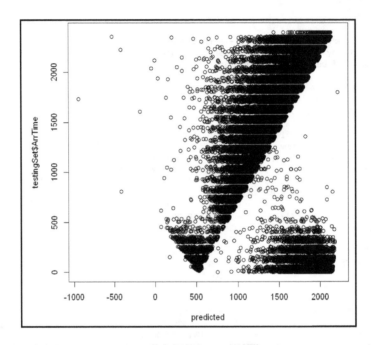

Visually, the predictions match up well with the actuals as shown by the almost 45 degree line. That whole set of predicted points on the lower-right portion of the graphic is troublesome. There appears to be many predictions that are well below the actuals. There must be additional factors involved, as I would have expected all of the data to plot in one area rather than two.

Summary

In this chapter, we first set up R as one of the engines available for a notebook. Then we used some rudimentary R to analyze voter demographics for the presidential election. We looked at voter registration versus actual voting. Next, we analyzed the trend in college admissions. Finally, we looked at using a predictive model to determine whether flights would be delayed or not.

In the next chapter, we will look into wrangling data in different ways under Jupyter.

6
Data Wrangling

In this chapter, we look at data in several different forms and pry useful statistics. The tools to access the data have been well developed and allow for data to be missing headings or data points in some of the records.

Reading a CSV file

One of the standards for file formats is CSV. In this section, we will walk through the process of reading a CSV and adjusting the dataset to arrive at some conclusions about the data. The data I am using is from the Heating System Choice in California Houses dataset, found at `https://vincentarelbundock.github.io/Rdatasets/datasets.html`:

```
#read in the CSV file as available on the site
heating <- read.csv(file="Documents/heating.csv", header=TRUE, sep=",")
# make sure the data is laid out the way we expect
head(heating)
```

X	idcase	depvar	ic.gc	ic.gr	ic.ec	ic.er	ic.hp	oc.gc	oc.gr	...	oc.hp	income
1	1	gc	866.00	962.64	859.90	995.76	1135.50	199.69	151.72	...	237.88	7
2	2	gc	727.93	758.89	796.82	894.69	968.90	168.66	168.66	...	199.19	5
3	3	gc	599.48	783.05	719.86	900.11	1048.30	165.58	137.80	...	171.47	4
4	4	er	835.17	793.06	761.25	831.04	1048.70	180.88	147.14	...	222.95	2
5	5	er	755.59	846.29	858.86	985.64	883.05	174.91	138.90	...	178.49	2
6	6	gc	666.11	841.71	693.74	862.56	859.18	135.67	140.97	...	209.27	6

The data appears to be as expected; however, a number of the columns have acronym names and are somewhat duplicated. Let us change the names of interest that we want to be more readable and remove the extras we are not going to use:

```
# change the column names to be more readable
colnames(heating)[colnames(heating)=="depvar"] <- "system"
colnames(heating)[colnames(heating)=="ic.gc"] <- "install_cost"
colnames(heating)[colnames(heating)=="oc.gc"] <- "annual_cost"
colnames(heating)[colnames(heating)=="pb.gc"] <- "ratio_annual_install"

# remove columns which are not used
heating$idcase <- NULL
heating$ic.gr <- NULL
heating$ic.ec <- NULL
heating$ic.hp <- NULL
heating$ic.er <- NULL
heating$oc.gr <- NULL
heating$oc.ec <- NULL
heating$oc.hp <- NULL
heating$oc.er <- NULL
heating$pb.gr <- NULL
heating$pb.ec <- NULL
heating$pb.er <- NULL
heating$pb.hp <- NULL

# check the data layout again now that we have made changes
head(heating)
```

X	system	install_cost	annual_cost	income	agehed	rooms	region	ratio_annual_install
1	gc	866.00	199.69	7	25	6	ncostl	4.336722
2	gc	727.93	168.66	5	60	5	scostl	4.315961
3	gc	599.48	165.58	4	65	2	ncostl	3.620486
4	er	835.17	180.88	2	50	4	scostl	4.617260
5	er	755.59	174.91	2	25	6	valley	4.319879
6	gc	666.11	135.67	6	65	7	scostl	4.909781

Now that we have a tighter dataset, let us start to look over the data:

```
# get rough statistics on the data
summary(heating)
```

```
       X          system    install_cost      annual_cost          income
 Min.   :  1.0   ec: 64   Min.   : 431.8   Min.   : 84.02   Min.   :2.000
 1st Qu.:225.8   er: 84   1st Qu.: 696.3   1st Qu.:155.75   1st Qu.:3.000
 Median :450.5   gc:573   Median : 778.5   Median :172.10   Median :5.000
 Mean   :450.5   gr:129   Mean   : 776.8   Mean   :172.12   Mean   :4.641
 3rd Qu.:675.2   hp: 50   3rd Qu.: 855.3   3rd Qu.:189.18   3rd Qu.:6.000
 Max.   :900.0            Max.   :1158.9   Max.   :248.43   Max.   :7.000
     agehed           rooms          region    ratio_annual_install
 Min.   :20.00   Min.   :2.000   mountn:102   Min.   :3.146
 1st Qu.:30.00   1st Qu.:3.000   ncostl:260   1st Qu.:4.193
 Median :45.00   Median :4.000   scostl:361   Median :4.504
 Mean   :42.94   Mean   :4.424   valley:177   Mean   :4.548
 3rd Qu.:55.00   3rd Qu.:6.000                3rd Qu.:4.854
 Max.   :65.00   Max.   :7.000                Max.   :8.646
```

Some points pop out from the summary:

- There are five different types of heating systems, gas cooling being most prevalent
- Costs vary much more than expected
- The data covers four large regions of California
- The ration of the annual cost versus the initial cost varies much more than expected

It is not obvious what the data relationships might be, but we can use the R plot() function to provide a quick snapshot that shows anything significant:

```
plot(heating)
```

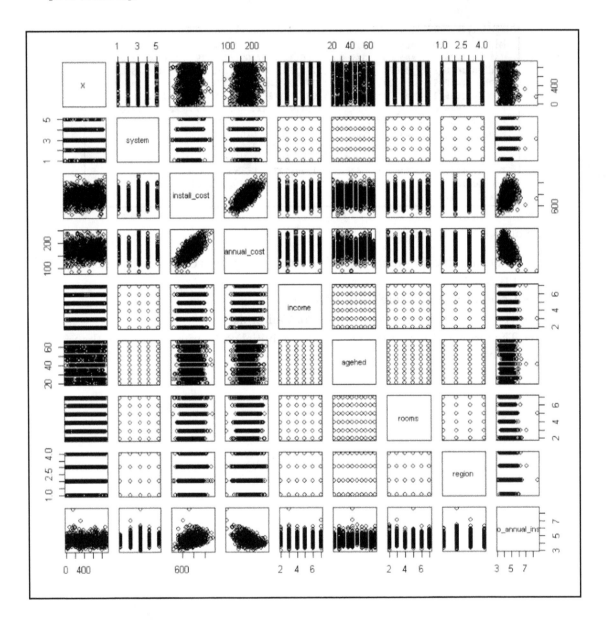

Again, several interesting facts jump out:

- The initial cost varies widely within the type of system
- The annual cost varies within the type of system as well
- Costs vary widely within the ranges of customer income, age, number of rooms in the house, and region

The only direct relationship between variables appears to be the initial cost of system and the annual cost. With covariance, we are looking for a measure of how much two variables change in relation to each other. If we run a covariance between the install and annual cost, we get:

```
cov(heating$install_cost, heating$annual_cost)
2131
```

I am not sure I have seen a higher covariance result.

Reading another CSV file

We can look at another CSV in the same dataset to see what kind of issues we run across. Using the yearly batting records for all Major League Baseball players that we previously downloaded from the same site, we can use coding like the following to start analyzing the data:

```
players <- read.csv(file="Documents/baseball.csv", header=TRUE,
sep=",")head(players)
```

This produces the following head display:

X	id	year	stint	team	lg	g	ab	r	h	...	rbi	sb	cs	bb	so	ibb	hbp	sh	sf	gidp
4	ansonca01	1871	1	RC1		25	120	29	39	...	16	6	2	2	1	NA	NA	NA	NA	NA
44	forceda01	1871	1	WS3		32	162	45	45	...	29	8	0	4	0	NA	NA	NA	NA	NA
68	mathebo01	1871	1	FW1		19	89	15	24	...	10	2	1	2	0	NA	NA	NA	NA	NA
99	startjo01	1871	1	NY2		33	161	35	58	...	34	4	2	3	0	NA	NA	NA	NA	NA
102	suttoez01	1871	1	CL1		29	128	35	45	...	23	3	1	1	0	NA	NA	NA	NA	NA
106	whitede01	1871	1	CL1		29	146	40	47	...	21	2	2	4	1	NA	NA	NA	NA	NA

There are many statistics for baseball players in this dataset. There are also many NA values. R is pretty good at ignoring NA values. Let us first look at the statistics for the data using:

```
summary(players)
```

This generates statistics on all the fields involved (there are several more that are not in this display):

```
       X                  id              year          stint
 Min.   :    4    mcguide01:  31   Min.   :1871   Min.   :1.000
 1st Qu.:27080    henderi01:  29   1st Qu.:1937   1st Qu.:1.000
 Median :48997    newsobo01:  29   Median :1970   Median :1.000
 Mean   :46655    johnto01 :  28   Mean   :1961   Mean   :1.093
 3rd Qu.:65780    kaatji01 :  28   3rd Qu.:1988   3rd Qu.:1.000
 Max.   :89534    ansonca01:  27   Max.   :2007   Max.   :4.000
                  (Other)  :21527

      team            lg               g                 ab                r
 CHN    : 1179    :    65   Min.   :   0.00   Min.   :   0.0   Min.   :   0.00
 NYA    : 1100   AA:   171   1st Qu.:  29.00   1st Qu.:  25.0   1st Qu.:   2.00
 SLN    : 1094   AL:10007   Median :  59.00   Median :131.0   Median :  15.00
 PHI    : 1070   FL:    37   Mean   :  72.82   Mean   :225.4   Mean   :  31.78
 CIN    : 1030   NL:11378   3rd Qu.: 125.00   3rd Qu.:435.0   3rd Qu.:  58.00
 PIT    : 1020   PL:    32   Max.   : 165.00   Max.   :705.0   Max.   : 177.00
 (Other):15206   UA:     9

       h               X2b               X3b               hr
 Min.   :  0.00   Min.   :  0.00   Min.   :  0.000   Min.   :  0.000
 1st Qu.:  4.00   1st Qu.:  0.00   1st Qu.:  0.000   1st Qu.:  0.000
 Median : 32.00   Median :  5.00   Median :  1.000   Median :  1.000
 Mean   : 61.76   Mean   : 10.45   Mean   :  2.194   Mean   :  5.234
 3rd Qu.:119.00   3rd Qu.: 19.00   3rd Qu.:  3.000   3rd Qu.:  7.000
 Max.   :257.00   Max.   : 64.00   Max.   : 28.000   Max.   : 73.000
```

A number of interesting points are visible in the preceding display that are worth noting:

- We have about 30 data points per player
- It is interesting that the player data goes back to 1871
- There are about 1,000 data points per team
- American League and National League are clearly more popular
- The range of some of the data points is surprising:
    - At bats range from 0 to 700
    - Runs (r) range from 0 to 177
    - Hits (h) range from 0 to 257

If we just plot some of the dominant data points, we can see the following:

```
plot(players$h, type="l", col="blue")

# doubles
lines(players$X2b, type="l", col="yellow")

# home runs
lines(players$hr, type="l", col="green")

# triples
lines(players$X3b, type="l", col="red")

# Create a title with a red, bold/italic font
title(main="Hits", font.main=4)#, xlab="Players", ylab="Hits and Home
Runs")
```

 The statistic graphs are displayed in this order so that smaller values are not overwritten by larger values (for example, the hits (largest numbers) are displayed first and the triples (smallest numbers) are displayed last on top of the previous numbers).

We have a display of the types of hits made by players over time as follows.

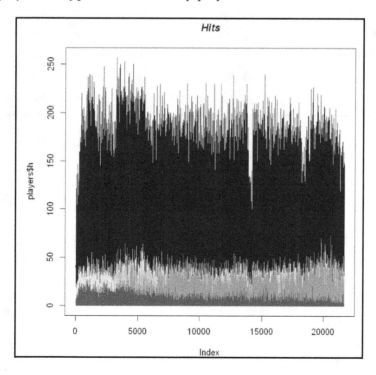

I thought it was interesting that so few triples were hit. Also, since the data is organized somewhat chronologically, the number of triples that are hit has been decreasing for some time. Maybe there is an emphasis on batting to go for the home run over batting to get a triple.

Manipulating data with dplyr

The `dplyr` package for R is described as a package providing a grammar for data manipulation. It has the entry points you would expect for wrangling your data frame in one package. We will use the `dplyr` package against the baseball player statistics we used earlier in this chapter.

We read in the player data and show the first few rows:

```
players <- read.csv(file="Documents/baseball.csv", header=TRUE, sep=",")
head(players)
```

X	id	year	stint	team	lg	g	ab	r	h	...	rbi	sb	cs	bb	so	ibb	hbp	sh	sf	gidp
4	ansonca01	1871	1	RC1		25	120	29	39	...	16	6	2	2	1	NA	NA	NA	NA	NA
44	forceda01	1871	1	WS3		32	162	45	45	...	29	8	0	4	0	NA	NA	NA	NA	NA
68	mathebo01	1871	1	FW1		19	89	15	24	...	10	2	1	2	0	NA	NA	NA	NA	NA
99	startjo01	1871	1	NY2		33	161	35	58	...	34	4	2	3	0	NA	NA	NA	NA	NA
102	suttoez01	1871	1	CL1		29	128	35	45	...	23	3	1	1	0	NA	NA	NA	NA	NA
106	whitede01	1871	1	CL1		29	146	40	47	...	21	2	2	4	1	NA	NA	NA	NA	NA

We will be using the `dplyr` package, so we need to pull the package into our notebook:

```
library(dplyr)
```

Converting a data frame to a dplyr table

The `dplyr` package has functions to convert your data object into a `dplyr` table. A `dplyr` table stores data in a compact format using much less memory. Most of the other `dplyr` functions can operate directly on the table as well.

We can convert our data frame to a table using:

```
playerst <- tbl_df(players) playerst
```

This results in a very similar display pattern:

X	id	year	stint	team	lg	g	ab	r	h	...	rbi	sb	cs	bb	so	ibb	hbp	sh	sf	gidp
4	ansonca01	1871	1	RC1		25	120	29	39	...	16	6	2	2	1	NA	NA	NA	NA	NA
44	forceda01	1871	1	WS3		32	162	45	45	...	29	8	0	4	0	NA	NA	NA	NA	NA
68	mathebo01	1871	1	FW1		19	89	15	24	...	10	2	1	2	0	NA	NA	NA	NA	NA
99	startjo01	1871	1	NY2		33	161	35	58	...	34	4	2	3	0	NA	NA	NA	NA	NA
102	suttoez01	1871	1	CL1		29	128	35	45	...	23	3	1	1	0	NA	NA	NA	NA	NA
106	whitede01	1871	1	CL1		29	146	40	47	...	21	2	2	4	1	NA	NA	NA	NA	NA
113	yorkto01	1871	1	TRO		29	145	36	37	...	23	2	2	9	1	NA	NA	NA	NA	NA
121	ansonca01	1872	1	PH1		46	217	60	90	...	50	6	6	16	3	NA	NA	NA	NA	NA

Getting a quick overview of the data value ranges

Another function available in `dplyr` is the `glimpse()` function. It takes every column and displays the range of values present for that variable. We use the function in the following way:

```
glimpse(playerst)
```

This has the following display:

```
Observations: 21,699
Variables: 23
$ X     <int> 4, 44, 68, 99, 102, 106, 113, 121, 143, 167, 168, 186, 209, 2...
$ id    <fctr> ansonca01, forceda01, mathebo01, startjo01, suttoez01, white...
$ year  <int> 1871, 1871, 1871, 1871, 1871, 1871, 1871, 1872, 1872, 1872, 1...
$ stint <int> 1, 1, 1, 1, 1, 1, 1, 1, 1, 1, 2, 1, 1, 1, 2, 1, 1, 1, 1, 1, 1...
$ team  <fctr> RC1, WS3, FW1, NY2, CL1, CL1, TRO, PH1, BR2, TRO, BL1, WS4, ...
$ lg    <fctr> , , , , , , , , , , , , , , , , , , , , , , , ,
$ g     <int> 25, 32, 19, 33, 29, 29, 29, 46, 37, 25, 19, 11, 50, 4, 18, 23...
$ ab    <int> 120, 162, 89, 161, 128, 146, 145, 217, 174, 130, 95, 49, 223,...
$ r     <int> 29, 45, 15, 35, 35, 40, 36, 60, 26, 40, 29, 9, 36, 2, 12, 25,...
$ h     <int> 39, 45, 24, 58, 45, 47, 37, 90, 46, 53, 41, 12, 50, 7, 19, 31...
$ X2b   <int> 11, 9, 3, 5, 3, 6, 5, 10, 3, 11, 2, 1, 1, 0, 2, 4, 4, 6, 2, 1...
$ X3b   <int> 3, 4, 1, 1, 7, 5, 7, 7, 0, 0, 2, 0, 0, 0, 0, 1, 0, 1, 2, 4, 2...
$ hr    <int> 0, 0, 0, 1, 3, 1, 2, 0, 0, 0, 0, 0, 0, 0, 0, 0, 0, 0, 0, 1, 0...
$ rbi   <int> 16, 29, 10, 34, 23, 21, 23, 50, 15, 16, 13, 5, 21, 4, 8, 12, ...
$ sb    <int> 6, 8, 2, 4, 3, 2, 2, 6, 0, 2, 3, 0, 1, 0, 1, 1, 3, 1, 0, 2, 0...
$ cs    <int> 2, 0, 1, 2, 1, 2, 2, 6, 1, 2, 0, 0, 1, 0, 0, 0, 3, 0, 0, 1, 2...
$ bb    <int> 2, 4, 2, 3, 1, 4, 9, 16, 1, 1, 1, 0, 3, 0, 2, 2, 0, 1, 4, 4, ...
$ so    <int> 1, 0, 0, 0, 0, 1, 1, 3, 1, 0, 0, 0, 2, 2, 2, 0, 0, 1, 1, 1, 1...
$ ibb   <int> NA, NA, NA, NA, NA, NA, NA, NA, NA, NA, NA, NA, NA, NA, NA, N...
$ hbp   <int> NA, NA, NA, NA, NA, NA, NA, NA, NA, NA, NA, NA, NA, NA, NA, N...
$ sh    <int> NA, NA, NA, NA, NA, NA, NA, NA, NA, NA, NA, NA, NA, NA, NA, N...
$ sf    <int> NA, NA, NA, NA, NA, NA, NA, NA, NA, NA, NA, NA, NA, NA, NA, N...
$ gidp  <int> NA, NA, NA, NA, NA, NA, NA, NA, NA, NA, NA, NA, NA, NA, NA, N...
```

I think I like this, in addition to the set of summary/head displays, as you get a feel for the variables involved rather than the rows involved, inverting the dataset.

Sampling a dataset

The dplyr package has a function to gather a sample from your dataset, sample(). You pass in the dataset to operate against and how many samples you want drawn, sample_n(), and the fraction percentage, sample_frac(), as in this example:

```
data <- sample_n(players, 30) glimpse(data)
```

We see the results as shown in the following screenshot:

```
Observations: 30
Variables: 23
$ X     <int> 3531, 49852, 83330, 44753, 29473, 43131, 48665, 62357, 74109,...
$ id    <fctr> mathebo01, reedro01, guarded01, jenkife01, troutdi01, burges...
$ year  <int> 1887, 1971, 2002, 1965, 1941, 1963, 1970, 1985, 1995, 1930, 1...
$ stint <int> 1, 1, 1, 1, 1, 1, 1, 1, 1, 1, 1, 1, 1, 1, 1, 1, 1, 1, 1, 1, 1...
$ team  <fctr> PH4, ATL, MIN, PHI, DET, PIT, SDN, CAL, CHN, CLE, SLA, DET, ...
$ lg    <fctr> AA, NL, AL, NL, AL, NL, NL, AL, NL, AL, AL, AL, NL, NL, AL, ...
$ g     <int> 7, 32, 4, 7, 40, 91, 139, 150, 50, 86, 110, 138, 65, 35, 139,...
$ ab    <int> 25, 74, 0, 1, 50, 264, 534, 520, 162, 265, 390, 492, 176, 16,...
$ r     <int> 5, 3, 0, 0, 5, 20, 79, 80, 24, 30, 56, 75, 19, 0, 71, 64, 80,...
$ h     <int> 5, 11, 0, 0, 9, 74, 156, 137, 31, 78, 93, 136, 43, 1, 138, 86...
$ X2b   <int> 0, 0, 0, 0, 1, 10, 34, 23, 2, 23, 13, 23, 10, 0, 12, 10, 29, ...
$ X3b   <int> 0, 0, 0, 0, 1, 1, 1, 1, 0, 2, 6, 3, 2, 0, 7, 3, 4, 4, 0, 0, 5...
$ hr    <int> 0, 0, 0, 0, 0, 6, 23, 20, 6, 2, 6, 24, 1, 0, 3, 0, 11, 0, 1, ...
$ rbi   <int> 0, 1, 0, 0, 5, 37, 89, 85, 14, 37, 58, 82, 20, 0, 58, 36, 91,...
$ sb    <int> 0, 0, 0, 0, 0, 0, 5, 5, 0, 2, 0, 3, 1, 0, 7, NA, 9, 10, 1, 0,...
$ cs    <int> NA, 0, 0, 0, 0, 1, 3, 3, 0, 3, 5, 2, 0, NA, 7, NA, 5, NA, 0, ...
$ bb    <int> 4, 0, 0, 0, 4, 24, 34, 78, 36, 18, 24, 76, 15, 0, 61, 9, 91, ...
$ so    <int> NA, 20, 0, 1, 10, 14, 78, 61, 51, 17, 37, 84, 18, 5, 65, 28, ...
$ ibb   <int> NA, 0, 0, 0, NA, 8, 8, 3, 1, NA, NA, 7, 3, NA, 0, NA, 6, NA, ...
$ hbp   <int> 0, 0, 0, 0, 0, 1, 0, 13, 1, 1, 1, 5, 0, 0, 1, NA, 2, 2, 2, 0,...
$ sh    <int> NA, 6, 0, 0, 0, 0, 3, 5, 0, 4, 3, 4, 1, 1, 13, NA, 1, 5, 0, 2...
$ sf    <int> NA, 0, 0, 0, NA, 4, 6, 4, 1, NA, NA, 3, 0, NA, 8, NA, 12, NA,...
$ gidp  <int> NA, 0, 0, 0, 1, 12, 14, 12, 8, NA, 7, 6, 2, 0, 9, NA, 11, NA,...
```

Note that there are 30 observations in the results set, as requested.

Filtering rows in a data frame

Another function we can use is the `filter` function. The `filter` function takes a data frame as an argument and a filtering statement. The function passes over each row of the data frame and returns those rows that meet the filtering statement:

```
#filter only players with over 200 hits in a season
over200 <- filter(players, h > 200)
head(over200)
nrow(over200)
```

X	id	year	stint	team	lg	g	ab	r	h	...	rbi	sb	cs	bb	so	ibb	hbp	sh	sf	gidp
3454	brownpe01	1887	1	LS2	AA	134	547	137	220	...	118	103	NA	55	NA	NA	8	NA	NA	NA
3765	thompsa01	1887	1	DTN	NL	127	545	118	203	...	166	22	NA	32	19	NA	9	NA	NA	NA
4370	glassja01	1889	1	IN3	NL	134	582	128	205	...	85	57	NA	31	10	NA	5	NA	NA	NA
5832	delahed01	1893	1	PHI	NL	132	595	145	219	...	146	37	NA	47	20	NA	10	NA	NA	NA
5841	duffyhu01	1893	1	BSN	NL	131	560	147	203	...	118	44	NA	50	13	NA	1	NA	NA	NA
6023	thompsa01	1893	1	PHI	NL	131	600	130	222	...	126	18	NA	50	17	NA	6	NA	NA	NA

274

it looks like many players were capable of 200 hits a season. How about if we look at those players that could also get over 40 home runs in a season?

```
over200and40hr <- filter(players, h > 200 & hr > 40)
head(over200and40hr)
nrow(over200and40hr)
```

X	id	year	stint	team	lg	g	ab	r	h	...	rbi	sb	cs	bb	so	ibb	hbp	sh	sf	gidp
18834	ruthba01	1921	1	NYA	AL	152	540	177	204	...	171	17	13	145	81	NA	4	4	NA	NA
19528	hornsro01	1922	1	SLN	NL	154	623	141	250	...	152	17	12	65	50	NA	1	15	NA	NA
19883	ruthba01	1923	1	NYA	AL	152	522	151	205	...	131	17	21	170	93	NA	4	3	NA	NA
21925	gehrilo01	1927	1	NYA	AL	155	584	149	218	...	175	10	8	109	84	NA	3	21	NA	NA
23312	kleinch01	1929	1	PHI	NL	149	616	126	219	...	145	5	NA	54	61	NA	0	9	NA	NA
23524	gehrilo01	1930	1	NYA	AL	154	581	143	220	...	174	12	14	101	63	NA	3	18	NA	NA

16

It's a very small list. I know that player names are somewhat mangled, but you can recognize a few, such as Babe Ruth.

I wonder if any of the players hit over 300 times in a season.

```
filter(players, h > 300)
```

```
Warning message in cbind(parts$left, ellip_h, parts$right, deparse.level = 0L):
"number of rows of result is not a multiple of vector length (arg 2)"Warning message in cbind(parts$l
eft, ellip_h, parts$right, deparse.level = 0L):
"number of rows of result is not a multiple of vector length (arg 2)"Warning message in cbind(parts$l
eft, ellip_h, parts$right, deparse.level = 0L):
"number of rows of result is not a multiple of vector length (arg 2)"Warning message in cbind(parts$l
eft, ellip_h, parts$right, deparse.level = 0L):
"number of rows of result is not a multiple of vector length (arg 2)"

X  id  year  stint  team  lg  g  ab  r  h  ...  rbi  sb  cs  bb  so  ibb  hbp  sh  sf  gidp
```

It's interesting that no records met our `filter`, but the results handler requires a number of columns, and throws an error, as in this case there are none. Usually, errors in R are due to programming errors. It is unusual for R to generate an error for what I think would be normal no result data.

Adding a column to a data frame

The `mutate` function can be used to add a column to a data frame using the familiar R programming syntax you have seen elsewhere. In this case, we are adding a column to the data frame that has the percentage of time the player got a hit when at bat:

```
pct <- mutate(players, hitpct = h / ab) head(pct)
```

X	id	year	stint	team	lg	g	ab	r	h	...	sb	cs	bb	so	ibb	hbp	sh	sf	gidp	hitpct
4	ansonca01	1871	1	RC1		25	120	29	39	...	6	2	2	1	NA	NA	NA	NA	NA	0.3250000
44	forceda01	1871	1	WS3		32	162	45	45	...	8	0	4	0	NA	NA	NA	NA	NA	0.2777778
68	mathebo01	1871	1	FW1		19	89	15	24	...	2	1	2	0	NA	NA	NA	NA	NA	0.2696629
99	startjo01	1871	1	NY2		33	161	35	58	...	4	2	3	0	NA	NA	NA	NA	NA	0.3602484
102	suttoez01	1871	1	CL1		29	128	35	45	...	3	1	1	0	NA	NA	NA	NA	NA	0.3515625
106	whitede01	1871	1	CL1		29	146	40	47	...	2	2	4	1	NA	NA	NA	NA	NA	0.3219178

You can see the new column on the right in the preceding display. If we run a `summary`, we will get a summary of all fields (including the new `hitpct`):

```
summary(pct)
```

```
         hitpct
Min.    :0.0000
1st Qu.:0.1944
Median :0.2537
Mean    :0.2340
3rd Qu.:0.2887
Max.    :1.0000
NA's    :2178
```

With the max at `1.0`, that would mean some players got a hit every time they were at bat. Similarly, those with `0.0` never got a hit. It looks like a narrow range in the 20% area. Assume the `1.0` is one at bat and one hit, as all the other values are measured in multiple decimal points.

Obtaining a summary on a calculated field

We can arrive more directly at the summary value for the column using the `summarize` function. The function takes a data frame and a singular calculated result. We can see the same result using the script as follows:

```
summarize(pct, mean(hitpct, na.rm = TRUE))
```

mean(hitpct, na.rm = TRUE)
0.2339838

Piping data between functions

We can obtain the same results by *piping* the data between functions. Piping is denoted using the symbols `%>%` in R programming. It is available from the `magrittr` package. The piping symbols are normally thought of as synonyms for *then* in English. For example, the R statement `data %>% function()` means take the data object and then pass it along to the `function()`, just as if we had entered the statement `function(data)`.

To produce the same summary on a calculated field using piping, we would write the following (meaning take the `pct` dataset and then pipe it into the `summarize` function, and take the `hitpct` field and pipe it into the mean function):

```
library(magrittr) pct %>% summarize(hitpct %>% mean(na.rm = TRUE))
```

Obtaining the 99% quantile

We can look at the cut-off for the 99% mark using the `quantile()` function. Using the same sample data, we could use:

```
quantile(pct$hitpct, probs = 0.99, na.rm = TRUE)
```

This would have corresponding output:

```
99%: 0.470588235294118
```

So, the hit percentage of 47% is the cutoff for the 99% level of the data. Given that the three-quarter percentile was at 28% (as in the preceding `hitpct` graphic), there is quite a range of performance for that last quarter of data points—that is, there are some great baseball players.

We could get a list of those players in the top 25% of the hit percentage using:

```
top_players <- filter(pct, hitpct > 0.47)
top_players <- top_players[order(top_players$hitpct) , ]
head(top_players)
nrow(top_players)
198
```

 If the players are arranged by hit percentage in descending order, then the players with perfect hit ratios are displayed, but they all had under 10 at bats.

We can see the data points as follows:

	X	id	year	stint	team	lg	g	ab	r	h	...	sb	cs	bb	so	ibb	hbp	sh	sf	gidp	hitpct
44	23963	willicy01	1930	1	PHI	NL	21	17	1	8	...	0	NA	4	3	NA	0	0	NA	NA	0.4705882
63	33399	grothjo01	1948	1	DET	AL	6	17	3	8	...	0	0	1	1	NA	0	0	NA	0	0.4705882
82	41843	niemabo01	1961	1	SLN	NL	6	17	0	8	...	0	0	0	2	0	0	0	0	0	0.4705882
6	11265	tanneje01	1908	1	BOS	AL	1	2	0	1	...	0	NA	0	NA	NA	0	0	NA	NA	0.5000000
7	11644	jennihu01	1909	1	DET	AL	2	4	1	2	...	0	NA	0	NA	NA	0	0	NA	NA	0.5000000
8	12005	raganpa01	1909	1	CIN	NL	2	2	0	1	...	0	NA	0	NA	NA	0	0	NA	NA	0.5000000

So, we have 200 (198) players in the top 25% of our dataset, meaning that 1% of the players are in the top 25% of hit performance. I did not think the data would be that lopsided.

Obtaining a summary on grouped data

Okay, the preceding steps tell us something about individual players. There is always the argument that team X is always better than everyone else. What if we could get a hit percentage by team and compare the results?

In this example, we are grouping the players by team and then computing an average hit percentage for the entire team:

```
teamhitpct <- summarize(group_by(pct, team), mean(hitpct, na.rm = TRUE))
names(teamhitpct) <- c("team", "hitpct")
summary(teamhitpct)
```

```
     team          hitpct
 ALT    : 1    Min.   :0.0000
 ANA    : 1    1st Qu.:0.2295
 ARI    : 1    Median :0.2463
 ATL    : 1    Mean   :0.2477
 BAL    : 1    3rd Qu.:0.2729
 BFN    : 1    Max.   :0.4186
 (Other):126
```

So, who were the best teams ever? We can order the data by the teams' hit percentages (the -teamhitpct clause means that the results should be arranged in descending order) using:

```
teamhitpct <- teamhitpct[order(-teamhitpct$hitpct) , ] head(teamhitpct)
```

team	hitpct
CNU	0.4186047
PH1	0.3419050
TRO	0.3376216
BS1	0.3362452
RC1	0.3250000
CL1	0.3233259

I'm not sure what the CNU team is; I assume it is an earlier Chicago team. The others are recognizable as Philadelphia, Toronto, and Boston.

We can find the top percentile of teams using the quantile function that we used previously for player hit performance:

```
quantile(teamhitpct$hitpct, probs = 0.99)
```

This gives us the following result:

```
99%: 0.340577141193618
```

Comparing this to the previous table, we can see that only two teams (out of 130) are in the top performance group (which is about the 1% mark).

Tidying up data with tidyr

The tidyr package is available to clean up/tidy your dataset. The use of tidyr is to rearrange your data so that:

- Each column is a variable
- Each row is an observation

When your data is arranged in this manner, it becomes much easier to analyze. There are many datasets published that mix columns and rows with values. You then must adjust them accordingly if you use the data in situ.

`tidyr` provides three functions for cleaning up your data:

- `gather`
- `separate`
- `spread`

The `gather()` function takes your data and arranges the data into key-value pairs, much like the Hadoop database model. Let's use the standard example of stock prices for a date using the following:

```
library(tidyr)
stocks <- data_frame(
  time = as.Date('2017-08-05') + 0:9,
  X = rnorm(10, 20, 1), #how many numbers, mean, std dev
  Y = rnorm(10, 20, 2),
  Z = rnorm(10, 20, 4)
)
```

This will generate data that looks like this:

time	X	Y	Z
2017-08-05	20.12058	20.56542	17.55471
2017-08-06	20.51702	18.40603	16.00274
2017-08-07	19.90123	20.34891	20.20725
2017-08-08	19.95212	21.27073	15.75052
2017-08-09	20.18198	18.75737	23.01953
2017-08-10	18.08772	18.10624	14.54853

Every row has a timestamp and the prices of the three stocks at that time.

We first use `gather()` to split out key-value pairs for the stocks. The `gather()` function is called with the data frame that it will work with, the output column names, and the columns to ignore (`-time`). So we get a row with the distinct time, stock, and prices using the following:

```
stocksg <- gather(stocks, stock, price, -time)
head(stocksg)
```

This will generate the following `head()` display:

time	stock	price
2017-08-05	X	20.12058
2017-08-06	X	20.51702
2017-08-07	X	19.90123
2017-08-08	X	19.95212
2017-08-09	X	20.18198
2017-08-10	X	18.08772

The `separate()` function is used to split apart values that are in the same entry points.

We will use Dow Jones Index history about industrial prices from UCI (`https://archive.ics.uci.edu/ml/datasets/Dow+Jones+Index`):

```
dji <- read.csv("Documents/dow_jones_index.data")
dj <- dji[,c("stock","date","close")]
summary(dj)
head(dj)
```

We are only interested in the `stock`, `date`, and `close` columns.

stock		date		close	
AA	: 25	1/14/2011: 30		$33.07 :	3
AXP	: 25	1/21/2011: 30		$36.00 :	3
BA	: 25	1/28/2011: 30		$41.52 :	3
BAC	: 25	1/7/2011 : 30		$46.25 :	3
CAT	: 25	2/11/2011: 30		$12.31 :	2
CSCO	: 25	2/18/2011: 30		$14.25 :	2
(Other):600		(Other) :570		(Other):734	

stock	date	close
AA	1/7/2011	$16.42
AA	1/14/2011	$15.97
AA	1/21/2011	$15.79
AA	1/28/2011	$16.13
AA	2/4/2011	$17.14
AA	2/11/2011	$17.37

So, we have the date already gathered to start with (if we had disorganized data to start with, we would have used `gather` to organize it up to this point).

The `spread()` function will take the key-value pairs (from the `gather()` function) and separate out the values into multiple columns. We call `spread()` using the data frame containing our source date, the values to use for our columns, and the data points for each date/column. Continuing with our example, we can spread out all of the securities by date using:

```
prices <- dj %>% spread(stock, close)
summary(prices)
head(prices)
```

This results in the following `summary` display (shortened to just the first few securities):

```
      date            AA               AXP              BA              BAC
1/14/2011: 1    $14.72 : 1      $46.25 : 2      $69.10 : 1      $12.31 : 2
1/21/2011: 1    $15.23 : 1      $43.53 : 1      $69.23 : 1      $14.25 : 2
1/28/2011: 1    $15.28 : 1      $43.72 : 1      $69.38 : 1      $10.52 : 1
1/7/2011 : 1    $15.79 : 1      $43.82 : 1      $70.07 : 1      $10.68 : 1
2/11/2011: 1    $15.92 : 1      $43.86 : 1      $71.26 : 1      $10.80 : 1
2/18/2011: 1    $15.97 : 1      $44.17 : 1      $71.38 : 1      $11.28 : 1
(Other)  :19    (Other):19      (Other):18      (Other):19      (Other):17
     CAT             CSCO             CVX             DD              DIS             GE
$100.01: 1      $14.93 : 1      $101.00: 1      $50.29 : 2      $41.52 : 3      $18.82 : 2
$100.02: 1      $14.97 : 1      $102.10: 1      $48.35 : 1      $37.58 : 1      $17.97 : 1
$101.10: 1      $15.12 : 1      $102.39: 1      $49.57 : 1      $38.04 : 1      $18.32 : 1
$102.00: 1      $16.01 : 1      $102.57: 1      $49.76 : 1      $38.50 : 1      $18.43 : 1
$103.04: 1      $16.46 : 1      $102.80: 1      $49.78 : 1      $38.85 : 1      $18.49 : 1
$103.54: 1      $16.53 : 1      $102.88: 1      $49.80 : 1      $39.29 : 1      $19.25 : 1
(Other):19      (Other):19      (Other):19      (Other):18      (Other):17      (Other):18
```

It also results in the following `head` display, showing the prices of all the securities by date:

date	AA	AXP	BA	BAC	CAT	CSCO	CVX	DD	DIS	...
1/14/2011	$15.97	$46.25	$70.07	$15.25	$94.01	$21.21	$92.83	$49.80	$39.29	...
1/21/2011	$15.79	$46.00	$71.68	$14.25	$92.75	$20.72	$93.78	$48.35	$39.74	...
1/28/2011	$16.13	$43.86	$69.23	$13.60	$95.68	$20.93	$93.37	$50.29	$38.85	...
1/7/2011	$16.42	$44.36	$69.38	$14.25	$93.73	$20.97	$91.19	$49.76	$39.45	...
2/11/2011	$17.37	$46.75	$72.14	$14.77	$103.54	$18.70	$96.45	$54.58	$43.41	...
2/18/2011	$17.28	$45.53	$73.04	$14.75	$105.86	$18.85	$98.72	$55.98	$43.56	...

We can also similarly reorganize the data by listing all prices for a stock per row using:

```
times <- dj %>% spread(date, close)
summary(times)
head(times)
```

Here, our row driver is the stock, the column heading is the date value, and the data point for each stock/date is the closing price of the security on that date.

From the `summary` (abbreviated), we can see the following:

```
       stock        1/14/2011        1/21/2011        1/28/2011        1/7/2011         2/11/2011
AA      : 1   $46.25 : 2   $14.25 : 1   $13.60 : 1   $14.25 : 1   $103.54: 1
AXP     : 1   $15.25 : 1   $15.79 : 1   $159.21: 1   $147.93: 1   $14.77 : 1
BA      : 1   $15.97 : 1   $155.50: 1   $16.13 : 1   $16.42 : 1   $163.85: 1
BAC     : 1   $150.00: 1   $18.36 : 1   $18.15 : 1   $18.34 : 1   $17.37 : 1
CAT     : 1   $18.34 : 1   $19.74 : 1   $20.20 : 1   $18.43 : 1   $18.70 : 1
CSCO    : 1   $18.82 : 1   $20.72 : 1   $20.93 : 1   $20.66 : 1   $18.83 : 1
(Other):24   (Other):23   (Other):24   (Other):24   (Other):24   (Other):24
```

The following is the `head` sample showing the data in our desired format:

stock	1/14/2011	1/21/2011	1/28/2011	1/7/2011	2/11/2011	2/18/2011	2/25/2011	2/4/2011	3/11/2011	...
AA	$15.97	$15.79	$16.13	$16.42	$17.37	$17.28	$16.68	$17.14	$16.03	...
AXP	$46.25	$46.00	$43.86	$44.36	$46.75	$45.53	$43.53	$43.82	$44.28	...
BA	$70.07	$71.68	$69.23	$69.38	$72.14	$73.04	$72.30	$71.38	$71.64	...
BAC	$15.25	$14.25	$13.60	$14.25	$14.77	$14.75	$14.20	$14.29	$14.38	...
CAT	$94.01	$92.75	$95.68	$93.73	$103.54	$105.86	$102.00	$99.59	$100.02	...
CSCO	$21.21	$20.72	$20.93	$20.97	$18.70	$18.85	$18.64	$22.05	$17.95	...

Summary

In this chapter, we read in CSV files and performed a quick analysis of the data, including visualizations to help understand the data. Next, we considered some of the functions available in the `dplyr` package, including drawing a glimpse of the ranges of the data items, sampling a dataset, filtering out data, adding columns using mutate, and producing a summary. While doing so, we also started to use piping to more easily transfer the results of one operation into another operation. Lastly, we looked into the `tidyr` package to clean or tidy up our data into distinct columns and observations using the associated gather, separate, and spread functions.

In the next chapter, we will look at producing a dashboard under Jupyter.

7
Jupyter Dashboards

A dashboard is a mechanism to put together multiple displays into one for use in a presentation. For example, you can take 3 graphical displays of production lines drawn from different data and display them on screen in one frame or dashboard. With Jupyter we can draw upon many mechanisms for retrieving and visualizing data which can then be put together into a single presentation.

Visualizing glyph ready data

A glyph is a symbol. In this section, we are looking to display glyphs at different points in a graph rather than the standard dot as the glyph should provide more visual information to the viewer. Often there is an attribute about a data point that can be used to turn the data point into a useful glyph, as we will see in the following examples.

The `ggplot2` package is useful for visualizing data in a variety of ways. `ggplot` is described as a plotting system for R. We will look at an example that displays volcano data points across the globe. I used the information from the National Center for Environmental Information at `https://www.ngdc.noaa.gov/nndc`. I selected volcano information post-1964.

This generated a set of data that I copied into a local CSV file:

```
#read in the CSV file as available as described previously
volcanoes = read.csv("volcanoes.csv")
head(volcanoes)
```

Number	Volcano.Name	Country	Region	Latitude	Longitude	Elev	Type
1402-08=	Acatenango	Guatemala	Guatemala	14.501	-90.876	3976	Stratovolcano
0803-17=	Adatara	Japan	Honshu-Japan	37.620	140.280	1718	Stratovolcano
0604-02=	Agung	Indonesia	Lesser Sunda Is	-8.342	115.508	3142	Stratovolcano
1000-123	Akademia Nauk	Russia	Kamchatka	53.980	159.450	1180	Stratovolcano
0805-07=	Akan	Japan	Hokkaido-Japan	43.380	144.020	1499	Caldera
0803-23=	Akita-Komaga-take	Japan	Honshu-Japan	39.750	140.800	1637	Stratovolcano

If we just plot out the points on a world map we can see where the volcanoes are located. We are using the `mapdata` package for the map:

 The latest R syntax requires specifying the location of the repository (or mirror) to find the package as part of the `install.packages()` function call.

```
#install.packages("mapdata",repos = "http://cran.us.r-project.org")
library(maps)
map("world")
points(volcanoes$Longitude, volcanoes$Latitude, pch=16, col="red", cex=1)
```

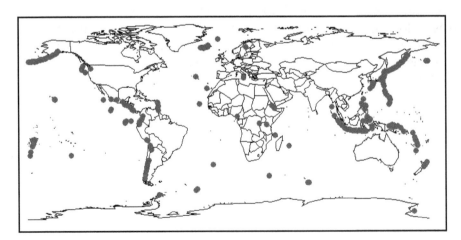

There are a few scattered volcanoes, but the dominating patterns are on the western Americas and southeast Asia, corresponding to the tectonic plate lines.

We can use some of the data points as glyphs and present that information in a similar graphic using the `qplot` (quick plot) function within `ggplot2`:

```
library(ggplot2)
qplot(Longitude, Latitude, data=volcanoes, color=Type, size=Elev, alpha=0.5)
```

The arguments are:

- x, y, `Longititude`, and `Latitude`
- Datasets we are referencing
- We are using color to connote the type of volcano
- The size of the data point corresponds to the elevation of the volcano
- Setting alpha at a mid-point will draw half-shaded color points so that we have a better visual of the overlaps

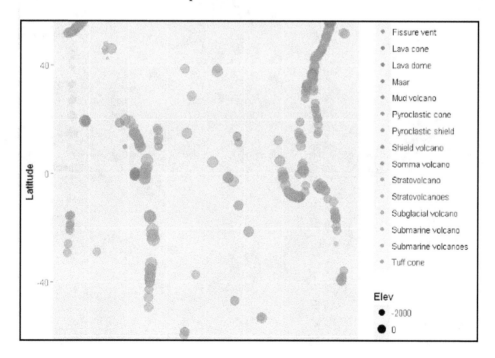

There may be a way to overlay the glyph data with the preceding geographic map.

The majority of the volcanoes are at over 2,000 feet elevation. Volcanoes in southeast Asia and the southern Pacific tend to be underwater.

Similarly, we can display glyph data about the standard `iris` dataset:

```
library(ggplot2)
qplot(Sepal.Length, Petal.Length, data=iris, color=Species,
size=Petal.Length)
```

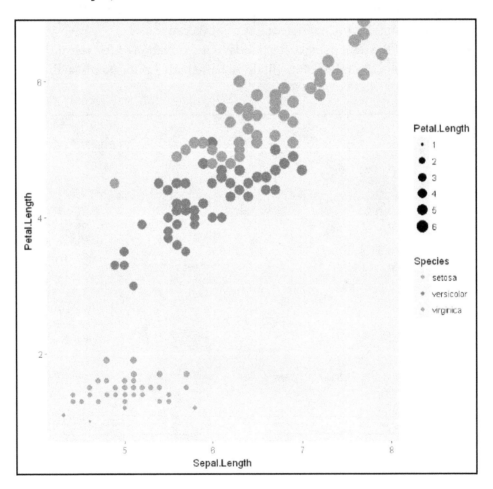

For the glyphs in this graphic we are using petal length and species. The graphics make it very clear that the species can be determined by the dimensions of the plant parts.

Or, using the diamonds built-in dataset, we can derive some information from the glyph data:

```
library(ggplot2)
dsmall <- diamonds[sample(nrow(diamonds), 100), ]

(d <- ggplot(dsmall, aes(carat, price)) + geom_point(aes(shape = cut))) +
scale_shape(solid = FALSE)
```

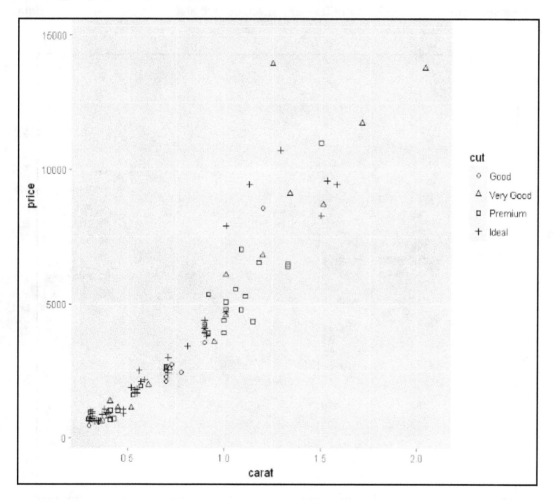

I had not expected the size (carats) to be the primary determinant of the price. I know everyone has been told or heard that the cut, clarity, and color make a difference, but the graph of actual data does not appear to show that those make any difference at all.

We can also look at the automobile miles-per-gallon dataset in a similar manner:

```
library(ggplot2)
ggplot(data=mpg) +
  geom_point(mapping = aes(x=displ, y=hwy, color=class, size=class))
```

In this example, we are mapping the aesthetic data points where x, y positions are based on engine displacement and highway miles per gallon, but we also `color` and `size` the data points based on vehicle class.

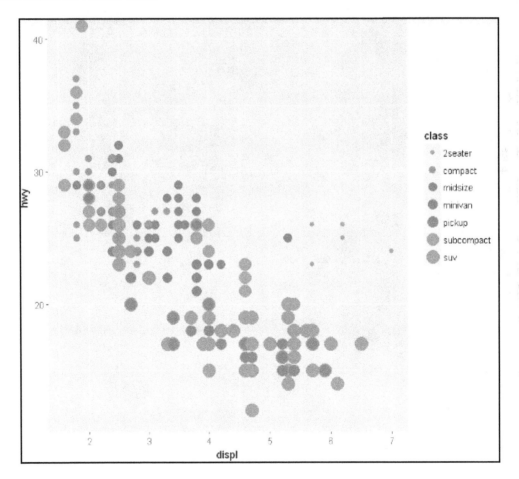

The glyphs make it clearer:

- SUVs have lower mileage regardless of engine displacement size
- Subcompact and compact vehicles have better mileage
- It is interesting that engine size makes little difference within any vehicle class on mileage

I know these are intuitive data points, but having the information confirmed using glyphs makes it very clear.

Publishing a notebook

You can publish a notebook/dashboard using markdown. Markdown involves adding annotations to cells in your notebook that are interpreted by Jupyter and converted into the more standard HTML representations that you see in other published materials.

In all cases, we create the cell with the markdown type. We then enter the syntax for markdown in the cell. Once we run markdown cells the display of the cell changes to the effective markdown representation. You should also note there is no line number designation for markdown cells, as there is no code executing in markdown cells.

Font markdown

You can adjust font style information using `italic` and `bold` HTML notations. For example, if we have the code format of a cell as follows. You can use markdown that has markdown tags for italics (`<i>`) and bold (`<b>`):

```
You can use markdown that has
<i>italic</i> and <b>bold</b> text
```

When we run the cell we see the effective markdown as:

> You can use markdown that has *italic* and **bold** text

List markdown

We can use lists such as the following, where we start an un-numbered list (we could have used `nl` for a numbered list) with two list items enclosed with the list item (`<li>`) tag:

```
In [ ]:  <ul>
             <li>list item 1</li>
             <li>list item 2</li>
         </ul>
```

When we run this cell the resulting markdown is displayed:

- list item 1
- list item 2

Heading markdown

A hierarchical set of headings is available, as in this example of markdown where Jupyter is paying special attention to heading notation using the sharp symbol #:

```
# Heading 1
# Heading 2
## Heading 2.1
## Heading 2.2
```

It is curious that Jupyter decided to specially handle this markdown versus any others.

With the resulting display:

Heading 1

Heading 2

Heading 2.1

Heading 2.2

Table markdown

We can generate tables, as in HTML. An HTML table starts with the `table` tag. Each row of the table starts with the `tr` tag. Columns within a row start with the `td` tag. Alternatively, you could use the column heading tag `th` instead of the `td` tag. In this example, we have a small table markdown:

```
<table>
    <tr>
        <th>column 1</th>
        <th>column 2</th>
    </tr>
    <tr>
        <td>1</td>
        <td>2</td>
    </tr>
</table>
```

With the resulting display:

column 1	column 2
1	2

Tables are centered by default in markdown. We could have changed the table to be left justified using more markdown. We could also have put borders around the cells of the table by adding the `'borders=1'` phrase to the `table` tag. Note that the column headings are bold by default.

Code markdown

It is sometimes useful to display actual code statements as markdown in our presentation. We do this by prefixing the code sequence with triple back quotes and the name of the language to interpret the coding. We turn off the coding using a trailing triple back quote, as seen in this example:

```python
print "Hello World"
```

With the resulting display corresponding to language-specific keyword highlighting:

```
print "Hello World"
```

More markdown

There are additional markdown notations for the following:

- Emphasis
- Math symbols, geometric shapes, horizontal lines
- Monospace font
- Line breaks
- Indentation
- Colors (including background)
- Graphic references (note to be sure these are still accessible if your markdown is remotely deployed)
- Internal and external links (same concern when deployed)

Creating a Shiny dashboard

Shiny is a web application framework for R. It does not require the user to code HTML. There are normally two sets of code: the server and the **user interface** (**UI**). Both sets of code work on top of a Shiny server. A Shiny server can reside on one of your machines or in the cloud (via several hosting companies).

The Shiny server code set deals with accessing data, computing results, obtaining direction from the user, and interacting with other server code set to change results. The UI code set deals with layout of the presentation.

For example, if you had an application that produced a histogram of data the server set would obtain the data and produce results, display the results, and interact with the user to change the result—for example, it might change the number of buckets or range of data being displayed. The UI code set would strictly be concerned with layout.

Shiny code does not run under Jupyter. You can develop the coding using RStudio. RStudio is an **integrated development environment (IDE)** for developing R scripts.

With RStudio you can develop the code sets for the `server.R` and `ui.R` components and then run them. Running a Shiny application will:

- Open a new browser window
- Use the coding to generate the corresponding HTML for your coding
- Display the generated HTML in the new browser window

Once your application is working you can also take the next step to deploy the application onto an R server on the internet, where you can share the associated URL to your application with other users.

R application coding

When you start RStudio you will see the (hopefully) familiar display as follows. There are four main windows in the display (going clockwise from the upper left):

- Source code window. In this window you enter the script for a particular R script file. Saving a file in the source code window will update the file stored on disk (and it is viewable in the files window).
- **Environment/History** window. In this window, any datasets that have been loaded or variables that have been established are displayed.
- **Files** window. In this window, the current sets of files are displayed (and are accessible by clicking on a file to pull it into the source code window).
- The execution window. In this window, actual commands are made to the R server.

For the simple example we will use `server.R` and `io.R` files very similar to the files on the Shiny web pages, for example.

The `app.R` file has the following commands:

```
## app.R ##
# load the shiny dashboard library
library(shinydashboard)
# create a dashboard with title, sidebar and body
ui <- dashboardPage(
  dashboardHeader(title = "Shiny dashboard"),
  dashboardSidebar(),
  dashboardBody(
    fluidRow(
      box(plotOutput("plot1", height = 250)),
```

```
    box(
      title = "Controls",
      sliderInput("slider", "Number of observations:", 1, 100, 50)
    )
  )
)
)
# when the server is called upon by system, will generate normalized data
and plot it
# further, every interaction with the user will rerun this set of code
generating new data
server <- function(input, output) {
  set.seed(122)
  histdata <- rnorm(500)
  output$plot1 <- renderPlot({
    data <- histdata[seq_len(input$slider)]
    hist(data)
  })
}
# start the application - this calls upon the browser to get output for
display
shinyApp(ui, server)
```

The UI file only establishes the layout of the page:

```
library(shinydashboard)
# only calls upon shiny to create a dashboard page with header, sidebar and
body
# each of these components is defined in the preceding app.R code.
dashboardPage(
  dashboardHeader(),
  dashboardSidebar(),
  dashboardBody()
)
```

If we run the app.R program in RStudio we end up with a page that looks like the following. There is a header section, sidebar, and body. The body contains the display and the slider control. We can run the application by selecting the app.R file in the source window and then clicking on the **Run App** button at the top of the source window. Clicking on the **Run App** button has the effect of entering the command runApp('shiny') in the console window (so you could have done that yourself instead). Once the application is running you will see a message in the console window such as **Listening on http://127.0.0.1:6142** where R decided to deploy your application on your machine.

In the resultant new browser window we can see our Shiny application displayed:

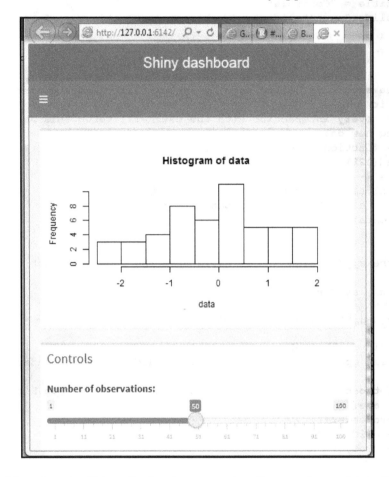

Note that the Shiny display is responsive. Responsive web applications will adjust the layout of components to accommodate changes in the physical size of the window. As in the previous display, you would expect the display to have the components laid out horizontally as they occur. As I changed the dimensions of the display to fit the printed page the layout got reorganized.

The page is fully active. As you move the slider the graphic gets regenerated.

Publishing your dashboard

Once you are satisfied with your dashboard you can publish it to the internet. The **Deploy** button near the top right of the source window will push your application set to the service that you connect.

In my case I used a free account with `http://www.shinyapps.io/`. There are other services available for hosting your Shiny applications.

Once you select to publish an application, RStudio will prompt you for the service and credentials to publish (credentials are provided to you when you enroll).

After that, the files are posted to your host and the application is up and running. As can be seen by hitting my demo account at `https://dantoomeysoftware.shinyapps.io/shiny` we get the exact same display as the preceding one, except that we are running on the hosted server.

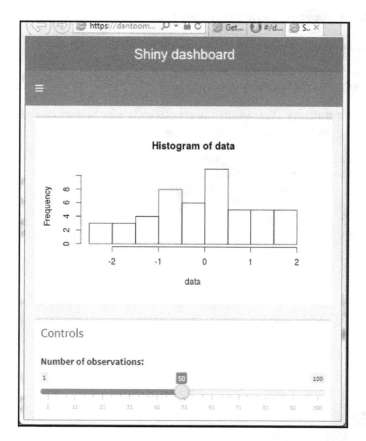

So, we have a easy to use system for creating our dashboard using a variety of display mechanisms. Overall, much easier than I expected—given my experience developing such presentations in other systems, such as Microsoft Tools.

Building standalone dashboards

Using Node.js, developers have come up with a way to host your dashboard/notebook without Jupyter on jupyter-dashboard-server.

Installation requires installing Node.js (as the server is written in Node.js). This is a larger installation set.

Once you have Node.js installed, one of the tools installed is npm-node product manager. You can use npm to install the dashboard server with the following command:

```
npm install -g jupyter-dashboards-server
```

Once installed you can run the server with the following command:

```
C:\Users\Dan>jupyter-dashboards-server --
KERNEL_GATEWAY_URL=http://my.gateway.com
```

mygateway.com is a dummy. You would use your gateway server (if needed). At this point the server is running on the environment you mentioned and will output a few lines:

```
Using generated SESSION_SECRET_TOKEN
Jupyter dashboard server listening on 127.0.0.1:3000
```

You can open a browser to the URL (`http://127.0.0.1:3000/dashboards`) and see what the server console looks like:

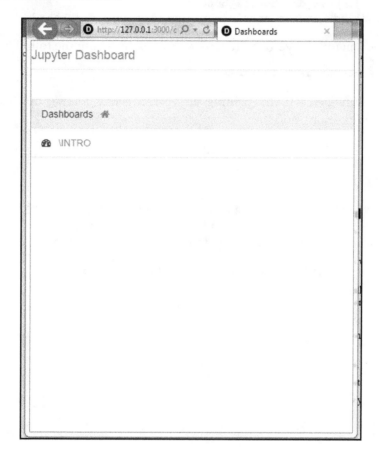

As for developing a dashboard you can host on the server, we need to install more:

```
conda install jupyter_dashboards -c conda-forge
```

Then enable the extension (it is a notebook extension):

```
jupyter nbextension enable jupyter_dashboards --py --sys-prefix
```

You then need to install the layout extension using the following commands:

```
pip install jupyter_dashboards_bundlers
jupyter bundlerextension enable --sys-prefix --py dashboards_bundlers
```

At this point you can upload your dashboard notebook file using the following command:

```
POST /_api/notebooks/[PATH/]NAME
```

Where the URL is prefixed with the hosting site you are using, PATH is optional (would default to the root location), and NAME is as you determine.

Summary

In this chapter, we visualized data graphically using glyphs to emphasize important aspects of the data. We used markdown to annotate a notebook page. We used Shiny to generate an interactive application. And we saw a way to host notebooks outside of Jupyter.

In the next chapter, we will look at statistical modeling under Jupyter.

8
Statistical Modeling

In this chapter we are taking raw data and attempting to interpret the information by building a statistical model. Once we have a model built then it is usually easier to see commonalities. We can determine trends as well.

Converting JSON to CSV

For this chapter, we will be using the Yelp data available from the challenge at `https://www.yelp.com/dataset/challenge`. This section uses the dataset from *round 9* of the challenge. For background, Yelp is a site for rating different products and services where Yelp publishes the ratings to users.

The dataset file is a very large (a few gigabytes) amount of ratings. There are several sets of rating information in the download-for business ratings, reviews, tips (as in this would be a nice place to visit), and a user set. We are interested in the review data.

When dealing with such large files it may be useful to find and use a large file editor so you can poke into the data file. On Windows, most of the standard editors are limited to a few megabytes. I used the Large Text File Viewer program to open these JSON files.

All of the files are in JSON format. JSON is a human readable format with structured elements—for example, a city object containing street objects. While it is convenient to read JSON the format is clumsy when dealing with large numbers of elements. In the `reviews` file there are a few million rows. So, we first convert the JSON to a flat CSV format to allow for easier processing using this script:

```
import time
import datetime
import json, csv
print( datetime.datetime.now().time())
```

```
headers = True
#with open('c:/Users/Dan/reviews.json') as jsonf,
open('c:/Users/Dan/reviews.csv', "wb") as csvf:
filein = 'c:/Users/Dan/yelp_academic_dataset_review.json'
fileout = 'c:/Users/Dan/yelp_academic_dataset_review.csv'
with open(filein) as jsonf, open(fileout, "wb") as csvf:
    for line in jsonf:
        data = json.loads(line)
        #remove the review text
        data.pop('text')
        if headers:
            w = csv.DictWriter(csvf, data.keys())
            w.writeheader()
            headers = False
        w.writerow(data)
print( datetime.datetime.now().time())
```

I am printing out the start and end times to get an idea of how long this takes. For my machine it took 1.5 minutes to convert the file. I had tried several versions of this code before I got the preceding code working at a satisfactory pace. While developing this script I took a small subset of the original data file (2000 rows) and worked with that file until things progressed sufficiently.

As you can see, I am reading the raw JSON file as provided from Yelp and writing out a corresponding CSV file.

The script reads each line of the JSON (one line contains an entire object) and writes out the corresponding CSV. I stripped out the review text as I was not evaluating the text of reviews and the review text took a lot of space. The review file size dropped from 3 gigabytes to 300 megabytes using this coding. Other than that we made sure to write the headers out to the CSV as the first record. I then used a separate script/notebook entry to read in the CSV and process it.

Evaluating Yelp reviews

We read in the processed Yelp reviews using this script and print out some statistics of the data:

```
reviews <- read.csv("c:/Users/Dan/yelp_academic_dataset_review.csv")
```

I usually take a look at some of the data once loaded to visually check that things are working as expected. We can do this with a head() function call:

```
head(reviews)
```

funny	user_id	review_id	business_id	stars	date	useful	type	cool
0	KpkOkG6RIf4Ra25Lhhxf1A	NxL8SIC5yqOdnlXCg18IBg	2aFiy99vNLklCx3T_tGS9A	5	2011-10-10	0	review	0
0	bQ7fQq1otn9hKX-gXRsrgA	pXbblgOXvLuTi_SPs1hQEQ	2aFiy99vNLklCx3T_tGS9A	5	2010-12-29	1	review	0
0	r1NUhdNmL6yU9Bn-Yx6FTw	wslW2Lu4NYylb1jEapAGsw	2aFiy99vNLklCx3T_tGS9A	5	2011-04-29	0	review	0
0	aW3ix1KNZAvoM8q-WghA3Q	GP6YEearUWrzPtQYSF1vVg	2LfluF3_sX6uwe-IR-P0jQ	5	2014-07-14	0	review	1
0	YOo-Cip8HqvKp_p9nEGphw	25RIYGq2s5qShi-pn3ufVA	2LfluF3_sX6uwe-IR-P0jQ	4	2014-01-15	0	review	0
0	bgl3j8yJcRO-00NkUYsXGQ	Uf1Ki1yyH_JDKhLvn2e4FQ	2LfluF3_sX6uwe-IR-P0jQ	5	2013-04-28	2	review	1

Summary data

All of the columns appear to be correctly loading. Now, we can look at summary statistics for the data:

```
summary(reviews)
```

```
       funny                         user_id
 Min.   :  0.0000    CxDOIDnH8gp9KXzpBHJYXw:    3327
 1st Qu.:  0.0000    bLbSNkLggFnqwNNzzq-Ijw:    1795
 Median :  0.0000    PKEzKWv_FktMm2mGPjwd0Q:    1509
 Mean   :  0.4195    QJI9OSEn6ujRCtrX06vs1w:    1316
 3rd Qu.:  0.0000    DK57YibC5ShBmqQl97CKog:    1266
 Max.   :632.0000    d_TBs6J3twMy9GChquEXkg:    1091
                     (Other)             :4142846
           review_id                      business_id
 ----X0BIDP9tA49U3RvdSQ:      1    4JNXUYY8wbaaDmk3BPzlWw:    6414
 ---0hl58W-sjVTKi5LghGw:      1    RESDUcs7fIiihp38-d6_6g:    5715
 ---30XpexMp0oAg77xWfYA:      1    K7lWdNUhCbcnEvI0NhGewg:    5216
 ---65iIIGzHj96QnOh89EQ:      1    cYwJA2A6I12KNkm2rtXd5g:    5116
 ---7WhU-FtzSUOje87Y4uw:      1    DkYS3arLOhA8si5uUEmHOw:    4655
 ---94vtJ_5o_nikEs6hUjg:      1    hihud--QRriCYZw1zZvW4g:    4120
 (Other)            :4153144    (Other)             :4121914
     stars              date             useful              type
 Min.   :1.000   2016-02-15:  3632   Min.   :   0.000   review:4153150
 1st Qu.:3.000   2017-01-15:  3600   1st Qu.:   0.000
 Median :4.000   2016-08-14:  3593   Median :   0.000
 Mean   :3.723   2016-04-03:  3588   Mean   :   1.008
 3rd Qu.:5.000   2016-07-31:  3566   3rd Qu.:   1.000
 Max.   :5.000   2016-07-10:  3559   Max.   :1125.000
                 (Other)   :4131612
      cool
 Min.   :  0.0000
 1st Qu.:  0.0000
 Median :  0.0000
 Mean   :  0.5262
 3rd Qu.:  0.0000
 Max.   :513.0000
```

There are several points in the summary worth noting:

- Some of the data points I had assumed would be just TRUE/FALSE, 0/1 have ranges instead; for example, `funny` has a max value over 600; `useful` has a max 1100, `cool` has 500.
- All of the IDs (users, businesses) have been mangled. We could use the user file and the business file to come up with exact references.
- Star ratings are 1-5, as expected. However, the mean and median are about a 4, which I take as many people only take the time to write good reviews.

Review spread

We can get an idea of the spread of the reviews using a simple histogram using:

```
hist(reviews$stars)
```

Which generates the histogram inline as:

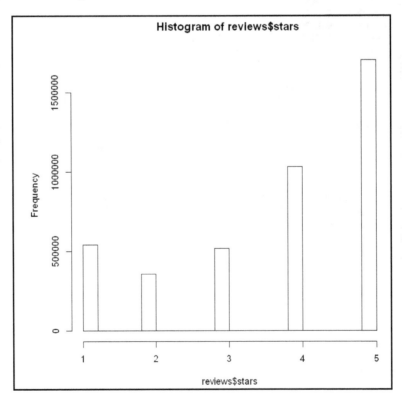

Again, we see the predilection for only making positive reviews (but the number of bad reviews is pretty large).

Finding the top rated firms

We can find the businesses with the most top ratings (5's) using the following script. This script uses SQL-like access to data frames. SQL has built-in mechanisms for searching and selecting and ordering of the data components as needed.

In this script we are building a computed data frame with two columns: business_id and review count. The data frame is ordered with the top rated firms appearing first. Once created, we display the head of the data frame to get at the top rated businesses in the dataset:

```
#businesses with most 5 star ratings
#install.packages("sqldf", repos='http://cran.us.r-project.org')
library(sqldf)
five_stars = sqldf("select business_id, count(*) from reviews where stars =
5 group by business_id order by 2 desc")
head(five_stars)
```

business_id	count(*)
hihud--QRriCYZw1zZvW4g	3115
4JNXUYY8wbaaDmk3BPzlWw	2774
DkYS3arLOhA8si5uUEmHOw	2330
RESDUcs7fliihp38-d6_6g	2230
cYwJA2A6I12KNkm2rtXd5g	2026
KskYqH1Bi7Z_61pH6Om8pg	1860

It is remarkable that the top five businesses had such a skewed amount of ratings (number 1 had close to double the number 6 business). You wonder if there is some collusion in the ratings process for such a divergence. Again, the names are mangled so far.

Finding the most rated firms

So, those companies had the most, best ratings. Which had the most ratings? We can use a similar script to determine the most rated firms:

```
#which places have most ratings
library(sqldf)
most_ratings = sqldf("select business_id, count(*) from reviews group by
business_id order by 2 desc")
head(most_ratings)
```

In this script we do not qualify the rating in order to determine its membership resulting in the set:

business_id	count(*)
4JNXUYY8wbaaDmk3BPzlWw	6414
RESDUcs7fliihp38-d6_6g	5715
K7lWdNUhCbcnEvl0NhGewg	5216
cYwJA2A6l12KNkm2rtXd5g	5116
DkYS3arLOhA8si5uUEmHOw	4655
hihud--QRriCYZw1zZvW4g	4120

So, similarly we see a small number of firms with many more ratings than average. Also, the names are mangled, but we do see four of the top-rated firms also being included in the most rated at all list.

Finding all ratings for a top rated firm

What if we looked at one of the top-rated firms to see where the ratings spread is? We could use the following script:

```
# range of ratings for business with most ratings
library(sqldf)
most_rated = sqldf("select * from reviews where business_id =
'4JNXUYY8wbaaDmk3BPzlWw' ")
hist(most_rated$stars)
```

The script takes one of the top rated IDs, accesses all of their ratings, and displays a histogram of the same:

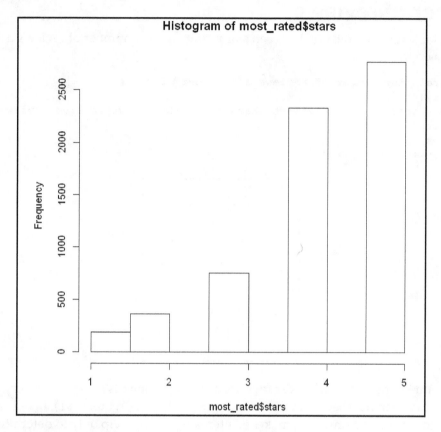

So, for one of the top rated firms there are very few low ratings.

Determining the correlation between ratings and number of reviews

We could look at the correlation between star rating and just number of reviews using the following script:

```
# correlation number of reviews and number of stars
library(sqldf)
reviews_stars = sqldf("select stars,count(*) as reviews from reviews group
by stars")
reviews_stars
cor(reviews_stars)
```

stars	reviews
1	540377
2	358550
3	517369
4	1032654
5	1704200

	stars	reviews
stars	1.0000000	0.8632361
reviews	0.8632361	1.0000000

So, we see three times as many 5 star reviews as 1 star reviews. We also see a very high correlation between number of reviews and number of stars (0.8632361). People are only bothering to rate good firms. That makes it interesting to use Yelp only to determine if the firm is reviewed at all. If the firm is not rated (or not rated much) the unwritten reviews are bad.

We could visualize the relationship between ratings and number of reviews for companies using the following script:

```
#correlation business and rating
library(sqldf)
business_rating = sqldf("select business_id, avg(stars) as rating from
reviews group by business_id order by 2 desc")
head(business_rating)
hist(business_rating$rating)
```

Where the `business_rating` data frame is a list of businesses and average star ratings. The resultant histogram is as follows:

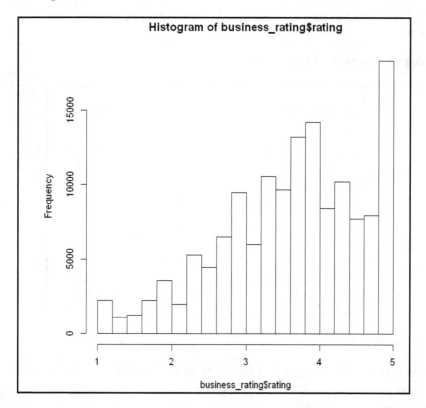

This looks like a Poisson distribution. It is interesting that the distribution of firm ratings takes such a natural dispersion.

Building a model of reviews

We can build a model from the dataset to estimate how many stars a rating may entail. However, the data points available within a review are only:

- funny
- useful
- cool

These would not appear to be good indicators for a rating number. We can use a model, such as:

```
model <- lm(stars ~ funny + useful + cool, data=reviews)
summary(model)
```

This produces the statistics of the model:

```
Call:
lm(formula = stars ~ funny + useful + cool, data = reviews)

Residuals:
    Min      1Q  Median      3Q     Max
-21.591  -0.773   0.227   1.227 101.763

Coefficients:
              Estimate Std. Error t value Pr(>|t|)
(Intercept)  3.7732752  0.0007266  5193.0   <2e-16 ***
funny       -0.1505152  0.0007393  -203.6   <2e-16 ***
useful      -0.1528960  0.0004952  -308.8   <2e-16 ***
cool         0.3169540  0.0007418   427.3   <2e-16 ***
---
Signif. codes:  0 '***' 0.001 '**' 0.01 '*' 0.05 '.' 0.1 ' ' 1

Residual standard error: 1.372 on 4153146 degrees of freedom
Multiple R-squared:  0.04644,   Adjusted R-squared:  0.04643
F-statistic: 6.741e+04 on 3 and 4153146 DF,  p-value: < 2.2e-16
```

As expected, we don't have enough information to work with:

- Over four million degrees of freedom, just about one per review
- *P* values are very small—the probability that we have estimated correctly is non-existent
- 3.7 intercept (close to the halfway point of the range)
- Such low affect rates (under one times each factor) meaning we aren't moving far from the intercept

Using Python to compare ratings

In the previous examples we used R to work through data frames that were built from converted JSON to CSV files. If we were to use the Yelp businesses rating file we could use Python directly, as it is much smaller and produces similar results.

In this example, we gather cuisines from the Yelp file based on whether the business category includes restaurants. We accumulate the ratings for all cuisines and then produce averages for each.

We read in the JSON file into separate lines and convert each line into a Python object:

 We convert each line to Unicode with the `errors=ignore` option. This is due to many erroneous characters present in the data file.

```
import json
#filein = 'c:/Users/Dan/business.json'
filein = 'c:/Users/Dan/yelp_academic_dataset_business.json'
lines = list(open(filein))
```

We use a dictionary for the ratings for a cuisine. The key of the dictionary is the name of the cuisine. The value of the dictionary is a list of ratings for that cuisine:

```
ratings = {}
for line in lines:
    line = unicode(line, errors='ignore')
    obj = json.loads(line)
    if obj['categories'] == None:
        continue
    if 'Restaurants' in obj['categories']:
        rating = obj['stars']
        for category in obj['categories']:
            if category not in ratings:
                ratings[category] = []
            clist = ratings.get(category)
            clist.append(rating)
```

Now that we have gathered all of the ratings, we can produce a new dictionary of cuisines with average ratings. We also accumulate a total to produce an overall average and track the highest rated cuisine:

```
cuisines = {}
total = 0
cmax = ''
maxc = 0
for cuisine in ratings:
    clist = ratings[cuisine]
    if len(clist) < 10:
        continue
    avg = float(sum(clist))/len(clist)
    cuisines[cuisine] = avg
```

```
    total = total + avg
    if avg > maxc:
        maxc = avg
        cmax = cuisine

print ("Highest rated cuisine is ",cmax," at ",maxc)
print ("Average cuisine rating is ",total/len(ratings))

print (cuisines)
```

```
Highest rated cuisine is  Personal Chefs  at  4.775
Average cuisine rating is  1.60022965191
{u'Whiskey Bars': 4.0, u'Acai Bowls': 4.115384615384615, u'Salvadoran': 3.888888888888889, u'Drugstores': 3.25, u'Tapas/Small P
lates': 3.8461538461538463, u'Amusement Parks': 3.45, u'Buffets': 3.0443661971830984, u'Performing Arts': 3.712121212121212,
u'Arts & Entertainment': 3.542307692307692, u'Cupcakes': 4.258620689655173, u'Curry Sausage': 3.8333333333333335, u'Pets': 3.5,
u'Shaved Ice': 4.162162162162162, u'Creperies': 3.8026315789473686, u'Canadian (New)': 3.4770606531881803, u'Belgian': 3.627906
976744186, u'Tea Rooms': 3.8285714285714287, u'Teppanyaki': 3.8157894736842106, u'Pretzels': 3.4423076923076925, u'Polish': 4.0
90163934426229, u'Dim Sum': 3.2886363636363636, u'Organic Stores': 4.113636363636363, u'Fitness & Instruction': 3.8823529411764
```

It is interesting that Personal Chefs is the highest rated. I have only heard about celebrities having a personal chef, but the data shows it may be worthwhile. An average of 1.6 is abysmal for all cuisines. The data did not appear to have a balance of high and low ratings when we looked earlier. However, looking through the resulting output, there are many items that are not cuisines, even though the Restaurants key is present. I had tried to eliminate the bad data by only counting cuisines with 10 or more ratings, which eliminated some of the bad data, but there are still many erroneous records in play.

Visualizing average ratings by cuisine

Now that we have the cuisine averages computed, we can display them in a histogram to get an idea of their spread. We first convert the dictionary to a data frame. Then plot the Rating column of the data frame into a histogram:

 We are using five bins to correspond to the five possible ratings.

```
import pandas as pd
import numpy as np
df = pd.DataFrame(columns=['Cuisine', 'Rating'])
for cuisine in cuisines:
    df.loc[len(df)]=[cuisine, cuisines[cuisine]]
hist, bin_edges = np.histogram(df['Rating'], bins=range(5))

import matplotlib.pyplot as plt
```

```
plt.bar(bin_edges[:-1], hist, width = 1)
plt.xlim(min(bin_edges), max(bin_edges))
plt.show()
```

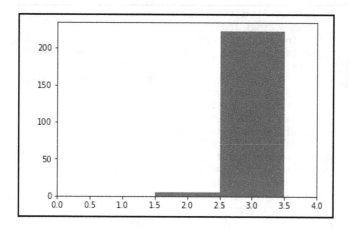

Again, we see a clear mark towards high average values. I had tried to get a better gradient on the data display to no avail.

Arbitrary search of ratings

Since we have the data in an easily loadable format we can search for arbitrary conditions, such as Personal Chefs that allow dogs-maybe they will custom cook for your dog.

We could use a script as follows: for line in lines:

```
line = unicode(line, errors='ignore')
obj = json.loads(line)
if obj['categories'] == None:
    continue
if 'Personal Chefs' in obj['categories']:
    if obj['attributes'] == None:
        continue
    for attr in obj['attributes']:
        print (attr)
```

Where we do something useful with the items that filter out. This script would display the attributes only for `Personal Chefs`. As can be seen in the following display:

```
BusinessAcceptsCreditCards: True
BikeParking: True
BusinessAcceptsCreditCards: True
BusinessParking: {'garage': False, 'street': True,
Caters: True
GoodForMeal: {'dessert': False, 'latenight': False,
RestaurantsDelivery: False
RestaurantsPriceRange2: 1
RestaurantsTakeOut: True
WheelchairAccessible: True
BusinessAcceptsCreditCards: True
RestaurantsPriceRange2: 2
RestaurantsPriceRange2: 4
BusinessAcceptsCreditCards: True
RestaurantsPriceRange2: 2
BusinessAcceptsCreditCards: True
BusinessAcceptsCreditCards: True
RestaurantsPriceRange2: 2
```

We could just as easily performed some calculation or other manipulation to narrow down and focus on a very specific portion of the data easily.

Determining relationships between number of ratings and ratings

Given the preceding results it appears that people mostly only vote in a positive manner. We can look to see if there is a relationship between how many votes a company has received and their rating.

First, we accumulate the dataset using the following script, extracting the number of votes and rating for each firm:

```
#determine relationship between number of reviews and star rating
import pandas as pd
from pandas import DataFrame as df
import numpy as np

dfr2 = pd.DataFrame(columns=['reviews', 'rating'])
mynparray = dfr2.values

for line in lines:
```

```
        line = unicode(line, errors='ignore')
        obj = json.loads(line)
        reviews = int(obj['review_count'])
        rating = float(obj['stars'])
        arow = [reviews,rating]
        mynparray = np.vstack((mynparray,arow))

    dfr2 = df(mynparray)
    print (len(dfr2))
```

This coding just builds the data frame with our two variables. We are using NumPy as it more easily adds a row to a data frame. Once we are done with all records we convert the NumPy data frame back to a pandas data frame.

The column names have been lost in the translation, so we put those back in and draw some summary statistics:

```
    dfr2.columns = ['reviews', 'rating']
    dfr2.describe()
```

In the output shown as follows we see the layout of the reviews and rating data we have collected. Yelp has not constrained its data entry for this dataset. There should 5 unique values for rating:

	reviews	rating
count	144072.0	144072.0
unique	951.0	9.0
top	3.0	4.0
freq	21912.0	29481.0

Next, we plot the data for a visual clue to the relationship, using the following:

```
#import matplotlib.pyplot as plt
dfr2.plot(kind='scatter', x='rating', y='reviews')
plt.show()
```

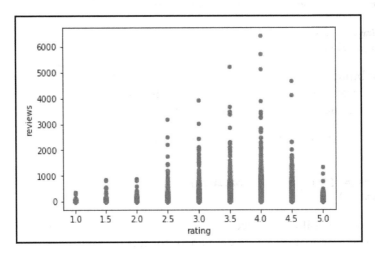

So, the data after all, appears to have a clear Poisson distribution as compared to the earlier `business_rating` histogram.

Next, we compute the regression parameters:

```
#compute regression
import statsmodels.formula.api as smf

# create a fitted model in one line
lm = smf.ols(formula='rating ~ reviews', data=dfr2).fit()

# print the coefficients
lm.params
```

	0	1	2	3	4	5	6	7	8
Intercept	0.044907	0.036966	0.037194	0.135542	0.065170	0.223576	0.074754	0.147955	0.233936
reviews[T.4.0]	-0.009818	-0.023913	0.068395	-0.095025	0.127464	-0.159860	0.177007	-0.093545	0.009295
reviews[T.5.0]	-0.020374	-0.015478	0.034054	-0.051506	0.080720	-0.086647	0.146299	-0.061048	-0.026019
reviews[T.6.0]	-0.028930	0.000092	0.018725	-0.035465	0.071855	-0.057039	0.082797	0.009151	-0.061185

We computed intercepts for all rating values. I had expected a single value.

Now, we determine the range of the observed data using the following:

```
#min, max observed values
X_new = pd.DataFrame({'reviews': [dfr2.reviews.min(), dfr2.reviews.max()]})
X_new.head()
```

	reviews
0	3.0
1	6414.0

So, as we guessed earlier, some businesses have a very large number of reviews.

```
Now, we can make predictions based on the extent data points:
#make corresponding predictions
preds = lm.predict(X_new)
preds
```

	0	1	2	3	4	5	6	7	8
0	4.490690e-02	3.696605e-02	3.719423e-02	1.355422e-01	6.516977e-02	2.235761e-01	0.074754	1.479555e-01	2.339357e-01
1	1.214306e-15	-4.579670e-16	1.582068e-15	3.830269e-15	9.575674e-16	5.884182e-15	1.000000	5.190293e-15	7.521761e-15

We are seeing a much bigger range of predicted values than expected. Plot out the observed and predicted data:

```
# first, plot the observed data
dfr2.plot(kind='scatter', x='reviews', y='rating')

# then, plot the least squares line
plt.plot(X_new, preds, c='red', linewidth=2)
plt.show()
```

In the plot displayed as follows, there does not appear to be a relationship between the number of reviews and the review score for a firm. It appears to be a numbers game—if you get people to review your firm, on average they will give you a high score.

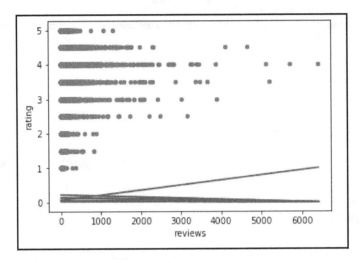

There does not appear to be a relationship between the number of reviews and the review score for a firm.

Summary

In this chapter, we used data and converted a JSON file to a CSV file. We evaluated the Yelp cuisine review dataset determining the top rated and most rated firms. We saw the distribution of ratings. We used Python to perform a similar evaluation of Yelp business ratings, finding very similar distributions of the data.

In the next chapter, we will look at machine learning under Jupyter.

9
Machine Learning Using Jupyter

In this chapter, we will use several algorithms for machine learning under Jupyter. We have coding in both R and Python to portray the breadth of options available to the Jupyter developer.

Naive Bayes

Naive Bayes is an algorithm that uses probability to classify the data according to Bayes theorem for strong independence of the features. Bayes theorem estimates the probability of an event based on prior conditions. So, overall, we use a set of feature values to estimate a value assuming the same conditions hold true when those features have similar values.

Naive Bayes using R

Our first implementation of naive Bayes uses the R programming language. The R implementation of the algorithm is encoded in the e1071 library. e1071 appears to have been the department identifier at the school where the package was developed.

We first install the package, and load the library:

```
#install.packages("e1071", repos="http://cran.r-project.org")
library(e1071)
library(caret)
set.seed(7317)
data(iris)
```

Some notes on these steps:

- The `install.packages` call is commented out as we don't want to run this every time we run the script.
- `e1071` is the naive Bayes algorithm package.
- The `caret` package contains a method to partition a dataset randomly.
- We set the `seed` so as to be able to reproduce the results.
- We are using the `iris` dataset for this example. Specifically, using the other `iris` factors to predict the species.

Invocations of the package look as follows:

```
model <- naiveBayes(response ~ ., data=training)
prediction <- predict(model, test, type="class")
```

Where the parameters to `naiveBayes` are:

- Formula of the form $y \sim x1 + x2$ ....-attempt to predict y based on $x1, x2, ...$
- Data frame
- Optional Laplace smoothing
- Optional subset of the data based on a Boolean filter
- Optional function for handling `na` values (`na.action`)—default is to pass

Once we have our model established we can then attempt a prediction using the `predict()` function with parameters for:

- Model (from the preceding call)
- Data frame
- Type whether the data is class or raw (conditionals)

So, we continue with the `iris` example with:

```
trainingIndices <- createDataPartition(iris$Species, p=0.75, list=FALSE)
training <- iris[trainingIndices,]
testing <- iris[-trainingIndices,]
nrow(training)
nrow(testing)
114
36
```

Where we split the data into 75% training and 25% for testing, as you can see by the number of rows in each data frame.

Next, we construct out model—we are trying to predict `Species` from the other features/columns of the data frame:

```
model <- naiveBayes(Species ~ ., data=training)
model
```

```
Naive Bayes Classifier for Discrete Predictors

Call:
naiveBayes.default(x = X, y = Y, laplace = laplace)

A-priori probabilities:
Y
    setosa versicolor  virginica
 0.3333333  0.3333333  0.3333333

Conditional probabilities:
           Sepal.Length
Y               [,1]      [,2]
  setosa     4.942105 0.3293167
  versicolor 5.950000 0.5371345
  virginica  6.602632 0.6598472

           Sepal.Width
Y               [,1]      [,2]
  setosa     3.371053 0.3805458
  versicolor 2.750000 0.2966024
  virginica  2.921053 0.2839470

           Petal.Length
Y               [,1]      [,2]
  setosa     1.468421 0.1662061
  versicolor 4.278947 0.4899850
  virginica  5.544737 0.5597767

           Petal.Width
Y               [,1]      [,2]
  setosa     0.2421053 0.1106042
  versicolor 1.3368421 0.1937134
  virginica  2.0000000 0.2438431
```

It is interesting that the Apriori assumption is an even split between the possibilities. Sepal length, width, and petal length have strong influences on species.

We make our prediction based on the model against the testing data:

```
prediction <- predict(model, testing, type="class")
```

Now, we need to measure the accuracy of the model. Normally we could use a scatter diagram using x from actual and y from predicted, but we have categorical data. We could build a vector of actual versus predicted and compare the two in a new results data frame:

```
results <- data.frame(testing$Species, prediction)
results["accurate"] <- results['testing.Species'] == results['prediction']
nrow(results)
nrow(results[results$accurate == TRUE,])
36
35
```

We end up with a model providing 97% (35/36) accuracy. This is a very good performance level, almost within the statistical boundary of excellent (+/- 2%).

Naive Bayes using Python

The Python implementation of the algorithm is in the `sklearn` library. The whole process is much simpler. First, load the `iris` dataset:

```
from sklearn import datasets
irisb = datasets.load_iris()
iris = irisb['data']
iris.shape
```

Call upon the built-in Gaussian naive Bayes estimator for a model and prediction in one step:

```
from sklearn.naive_bayes import GaussianNB
gnb = GaussianNB()
y_pred = gnb.fit(irisb.data, irisb.target).predict(irisb.data)
```

Determine the accuracy of the model:

```
print("Number of errors out of a total %d points : %d"
      % (irisb.data.shape[0],(irisb.target != y_pred).sum())))
Number of errors out of a total 150 points :  6
```

We end up with very similar results for estimation accuracy.

Nearest neighbor estimator

Using nearest neighbor, we have an unclassified object and a set of objects that are classified. We then take the attributes of the unclassified object, compare against the known classifications in place, and select the class that is closest to our unknown. The comparison distances resolve to Euclidean geometry computing the distances between two points (where known attributes fall in comparison to the unknown's attributes).

Nearest neighbor using R

For this example, we are using the housing data from `ics.edu`. First, we load the data and assign column names:

```
housing <-
read.table("http://archive.ics.uci.edu/ml/machine-learning-databases/housin
g/housing.data")
colnames(housing) <- c("CRIM", "ZN", "INDUS", "CHAS", "NOX", "RM", "AGE",
"DIS", "RAD", "TAX", "PRATIO", "B", "LSTAT", "MDEV")
summary(housing)
```

We reorder the data so the key (the housing price MDEV) is in ascending order:

```
housing <- housing[order(housing$MDEV),]
```

Now, we can split the data into a training set and a test set:

```
#install.packages("caret")
library(caret)
set.seed(5557)
indices <- createDataPartition(housing$MDEV, p=0.75, list=FALSE)
training <- housing[indices,]
testing <- housing[-indices,]
nrow(training)
nrow(testing)
381
125
```

We build our nearest neighbor model using both sets:

```
library(class)
knnModel <- knn(train=training, test=testing, cl=training$MDEV)
knnModel
10.5 9.7 7 6.3 13.1 16.3 16.1 13.3 13.3...
```

Let us look at the results:

```
plot(knnModel)
```

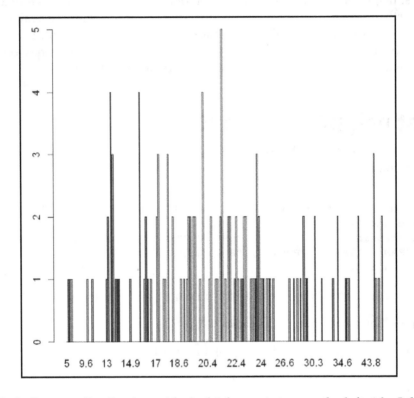

There is a slight Poisson distribution with the higher points near the left side. I think this makes sense as *natural* data. The start and end tails are dramatically going off page.

What about the accuracy of this model? I did not find a clean way to translate the predicted factors in the `knnModel` to numeric values, so I extracted them to a flat file, and then loaded them in separately:

```
predicted <- read.table("housing-knn-predicted.csv")
colnames(predicted) <- c("predicted")
predicted
```

predicted
10.5
9.7
7.0

Then we can build up a `results` data frame:

```
results <- data.frame(testing$MDEV, predicted)
```

And compute our accuracy:

```
results["accuracy"] <- results['testing.MDEV'] / results['predicted']
head(results)
mean(results$accuracy)
1.01794816307793
```

testing.MDEV	predicted	accuracy
5.6	10.5	0.5333333
7.2	9.7	0.7422680
8.1	7.0	1.1571429
8.5	6.3	1.3492063
10.5	13.1	0.8015267
10.8	16.3	0.6625767

So, we are estimating within 2% (`1.01`) of our testing data.

Nearest neighbor using Python

In Python, we have very similar steps for producing nearest neighbor estimation. First, we import the packages to be used:

```
from sklearn.neighbors import NearestNeighbors
import numpy as np
import pandas as pd
```

Numpy and pandas are standards. Nearest neighbors is one of the `sklearn` features. Now, we load in our housing data:

```
housing =
pd.read_csv("http://archive.ics.uci.edu/ml/machine-learning-databases/housi
ng/housing.data",
                   header=None, sep='\s+')
housing.columns = ["CRIM", "ZN", "INDUS", "CHAS", "NOX", "RM", "AGE", \
"DIS", "RAD", "TAX", "PRATIO", \
"B", "LSTAT", "MDEV"]
housing.head(5)
```

	CRIM	ZN	INDUS	CHAS	NOX	RM	AGE	DIS	RAD	TAX	PRATIO	B	LS
0	0.00632	18.0	2.31	0	0.538	6.575	65.2	4.0900	1	296.0	15.3	396.90	
1	0.02731	0.0	7.07	0	0.469	6.421	78.9	4.9671	2	242.0	17.8	396.90	
2	0.02729	0.0	7.07	0	0.469	7.185	61.1	4.9671	2	242.0	17.8	392.83	
3	0.03237	0.0	2.18	0	0.458	6.998	45.8	6.0622	3	222.0	18.7	394.63	
4	0.06905	0.0	2.18	0	0.458	7.147	54.2	6.0622	3	222.0	18.7	396.90	

The same data that we saw previously in R.
Let us see how big it is:

```
len(housing)
506
```

And break up the data into a `training` and `testing` set:

```
mask = np.random.rand(len(housing)) < 0.8
training = housing[mask]
testing = housing[~mask]
len(training)
417
len(testing)
89
```

Find the nearest neighbors:

```
nbrs = NearestNeighbors().fit(housing)
```

Display their indices and distances. Indices are varying quite a lot. Distances seem to be in bands:

```
distances, indices = nbrs.kneighbors(housing)
indices
array([[  0, 241,  62,  81,   6],
       [  1,  47,  49,  87,   2],
       [  2,  85,  87,  84,   5],
       ...,
       [503, 504, 219,  88, 217],
       [504, 503, 219,  88, 217],
       [505, 502, 504, 503,  91]], dtype=int32)
distances
array([[  0.        ,  16.5628085 , 17.09498324,18.40127391,
         19.10555821],
       [  0.        ,  16.18433277, 20.59837827, 22.95753545,
         23.05885288]
       [  0.        ,  11.44014392, 15.34074743, 19.2322435 ,
         21.73264817],
       ...,
       [  0.        ,   4.38093898,  9.44318468, 10.79865973,
         11.95458848],
       [  0.        ,   4.38093898,  8.88725757, 10.88003717,
         11.15236419],
       [  0.        ,   9.69512304, 13.73766871, 15.93946676,
         15.94577477]])
```

Build a nearest neighbors model from the `training` set:

```
from sklearn.neighbors import KNeighborsRegressor
knn = KNeighborsRegressor(n_neighbors=5)
x_columns = ["CRIM", "ZN", "INDUS", "CHAS", "NOX", "RM", "AGE", "DIS",
"RAD", "TAX", "PRATIO", "B", "LSTAT"]
y_column = ["MDEV"]
knn.fit(training[x_columns], training[y_column])
KNeighborsRegressor(algorithm='auto', leaf_size=30, metric='minkowski',
        metric_params=None, n_jobs=1, n_neighbors=5, p=2,
        weights='uniform')
```

It is interesting that with Python we do not have to store models off separately. Methods are stateful.

Make our predictions:

```
predictions = knn.predict(testing[x_columns])
predictions
array([[ 20.62],
       [ 21.18],
```

```
[ 23.96],
[ 17.14],
[ 17.24],
[ 18.68],
[ 28.88],
```

Determine how well we have predicted the housing price:

```
columns = ["testing","prediction","diff"]
index = range(len(testing))
results = pd.DataFrame(index=index, columns=columns)

results['prediction'] = predictions

results = results.reset_index(drop=True)
testing = testing.reset_index(drop=True)
results['testing'] = testing["MDEV"]

results['diff'] = results['testing'] - results['prediction']
results['pct'] = results['diff'] / results['testing']
results.mean()
testing         22.159551
prediction      22.931011
diff            -0.771461
pct             -0.099104
```

We have a mean difference of ¾ versus an average value of 22. This should mean an average percent difference of about 3%, but the average percentage difference calculated is close to 10%. So, we are not estimating well under Python.

Decision trees

In this section, we will use decision trees to predict values. A decision tree has a logical flow where the user makes decisions based on attributes following the tree down to a root level where a classification is then provided.

For this example, we are using automobile characteristics, such as vehicle weight, to determine whether the vehicle will produce good mileage. The information is extracted from the page at https://alliance.seas.upenn.edu/~cis520/wiki/index.php?n= Lectures.DecisionTrees. I copied the data out to Excel and then wrote it as a CSV for use in this example.

Decision trees in R

We load the libraries to use `rpart` and `caret`. `rpart` has the decision tree modeling package. `caret` has the data partition function:

```
library(rpart)
library(caret)
set.seed(3277)
```

We load in our `mpg` dataset and split it into a training and testing set:

```
carmpg <- read.csv("car-mpg.csv")
indices <- createDataPartition(carmpg$mpg, p=0.75, list=FALSE)
training <- carmpg[indices,]
testing <- carmpg[-indices,]
nrow(training)
nrow(testing)
33
9
```

We develop a model to predict `mpg` acceptability based on the other factors:

```
fit <- rpart(mpg ~ cylinders + displacement + horsepower + weight +
acceleration +
            modelyear + maker, method="anova", data=training)
fit
n= 33

node), split, n, deviance, yval
      * denotes terminal node

1) root 33 26.727270 1.909091
2) weight>=3121.5 10   0.000000 1.000000 *
3) weight< 3121.5 23 14.869570 2.304348
6) modelyear>=78.5 9   4.888889 1.888889 *
7) modelyear< 78.5 14   7.428571 2.571429 *
```

The display is a text display of the decision tree. You can see the decision tree graphically as follows:

```
plot(fit)
text(fit, use.n=TRUE, all=TRUE, cex=.5)
```

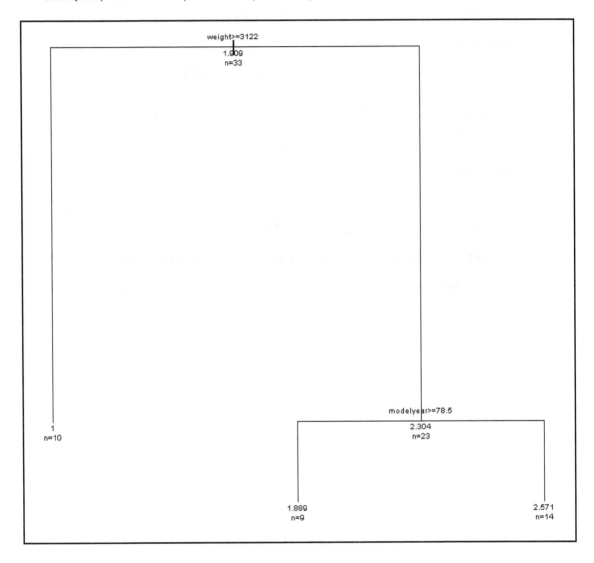

It appears to be a very simple model. There must have been a change to mileage for the 1980 year as that is the main driver for the decision tree.

Finally, we predict values and compare them against our `testing` set:

```
predicted <- predict(fit, newdata=testing)
predicted
testing
```

1	1
3	1
7	1
8	1
24	1.88888888888889
28	2.57142857142857
32	2.57142857142857
39	1.88888888888889
40	1.88888888888889

	mpg	cylinders	displacement	horsepower	weight	acceleration	modelyear	maker
1	Bad	8	350	150	4699	14.5	74	America
3	Bad	8	400	175	4385	12.0	72	America
7	Bad	6	250	105	3897	18.5	75	America
8	Bad	6	163	133	3410	15.8	78	Asia
24	OK	6	146	120	2930	13.8	81	Europe
28	OK	4	97	60	1834	19.0	71	Asia
32	OK	4	98	83	2219	16.5	74	Asia
39	Good	4	135	84	2370	13.0	82	America
40	Good	4	105	63	2125	14.7	82	America

It looks like the package has converted Bad, OK, and Good into a numerical equivalent where 1 is Bad and others are OK or Good. Overall, we are not sure if we have a good model. There is clearly not much data to work with. A larger test set would clear up the model.

Decision trees in Python

We can perform the same analysis in Python. Load a number of imports that are to be used:

```
import pandas as pd
import numpy as np
from os import system
import graphviz #pip install graphviz
```

```
from sklearn.cross_validation import train_test_split
from sklearn.tree import DecisionTreeClassifier
from sklearn.metrics import accuracy_score
from sklearn import tree
```

Read in the mpg data file:

```
carmpg = pd.read_csv("car-mpg.csv")
carmpg.head(5)
```

	mpg	cylinders	displacement	horsepower	weight	acceleration	modelyear	maker
0	Bad	8	350	150	4699	14.5	74	America
1	Bad	8	400	170	4746	12.0	71	America
2	Bad	8	400	175	4385	12.0	72	America
3	Bad	6	250	72	3158	19.5	75	America
4	Bad	8	304	150	3892	12.5	72	America

Break up the data into factors and results:

```
columns = carmpg.columns
mask = np.ones(columns.shape, dtype=bool)
i = 0 #The specified column that you don't want to show
mask[i] = 0
mask[7] = 0 #maker is a string
X = carmpg[columns[mask]]
Y = carmpg["mpg"]
```

Split up the data between training and testing sets:

```
X_train, X_test, y_train, y_test
= train_test_split( X, Y, test_size = 0.3,
random_state = 100)
```

Create a decision tree model:

```
clf_gini = tree.DecisionTreeClassifier(criterion = "gini",
random_state = 100, max_depth=3, min_samples_leaf=5)
```

Calculate the model fit:

```
clf_gini.fit(X_train, y_train)
DecisionTreeClassifier(class_weight=None, criterion='gini', max_depth=3,
          max_features=None, max_leaf_nodes=None,
          min_impurity_split=1e-07, min_samples_leaf=5,
          min_samples_split=2, min_weight_fraction_leaf=0.0,
          presort=False, random_state=100, splitter='best')
```

Graph out the tree:

```
#I could not get this to work on a Windows machine
#dot_data = tree.export_graphviz(clf_gini, out_file=None,
#                          filled=True, rounded=True,
#                          special_characters=True)
#graph = graphviz.Source(dot_data)
#graph
```

Neural networks

We can model the housing data as a neural network where the different data elements are inputs into the system and the output of the network is the house price. With a neural net we end up with a graphical model that provides the factors to apply to each input in order to arrive at our housing price.

Neural networks in R

There is a neural network package available in R. We load that in:

```
#install.packages('neuralnet', repos="http://cran.r-project.org")
library("neuralnet")
```

Load in the housing data:

```
filename =
"http://archive.ics.uci.edu/ml/machine-learning-databases/housing/housing.d
ata"
housing <- read.table(filename)
colnames(housing) <- c("CRIM", "ZN", "INDUS", "CHAS", "NOX",
                    "RM", "AGE", "DIS", "RAD", "TAX", "PRATIO",
                    "B", "LSTAT", "MDEV")
```

Split up the housing data into training and test sets (we have seen this coding in prior examples):

```
housing <- housing[order(housing$MDEV),]
#install.packages("caret")
library(caret)
set.seed(5557)
indices <- createDataPartition(housing$MDEV, p=0.75, list=FALSE)
training <- housing[indices,]
testing <- housing[-indices,]
nrow(training)
nrow(testing)
testing$MDEV
```

Calculate our `neuralnet` model:

```
nnet <- neuralnet(MDEV ~ CRIM + ZN + INDUS + CHAS + NOX
                  + RM + AGE + DIS + RAD + TAX + PRATIO
                  + B + LSTAT,
                  training, hidden=10, threshold=0.01)
nnet
```

The display information for the `neuralnet` model is quite extensive. The first sets of display are listed as follows. It is unclear if any of these points are useful:

```
$call
neuralnet(formula = MDEV ~ CRIM + ZN + INDUS + CHAS + NOX + RM +
    AGE + DIS + RAD + TAX + PRATIO + B + LSTAT, data = training,
    hidden = 10, threshold = 0.01)

$response
    MDEV
399  5.0
406  5.0
...
$covariate
          [,1]   [,2]  [,3] [,4]  [,5]  [,6]  [,7]   [,8] [,9] [,10]
[,11]
  [1,] 38.35180  0.0 18.10    0 0.6930 5.453 100.0 1.4896   24   666
20.2
  [2,] 67.92080  0.0 18.10    0 0.6930 5.683 100.0 1.4254   24   666
20.2
  [3,]  9.91655  0.0 18.10    0 0.6930 5.852  77.8 1.5004   24   666
20.2
....
```

Display the model:

```
plot(nnet, rep="best")
```

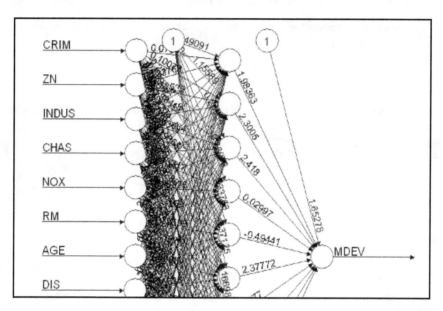

This is just the top half of the graph. As you can see, every factor is adjusted into the model to arrive at our housing price. This is not useful—every factor cannot be that important. Determine how accurate we are with this model:

```
results <- compute(nnet, testing[,-14])
diff <- results$net.result - testing$MDEV
sum( (diff - mean(diff) )^2 ) #sum of squares
9275.74672
```

Given the model appears to be very inaccurate I am not sure going through the same steps in Python would be beneficial.

Random forests

The random forests algorithm attempts a number of random decision trees and provides the tree that works best within the parameters used to drive the model.

Random forests in R

With R we include the packages we are going to use:

```
install.packages("randomForest", repos="http://cran.r-project.org")
library(randomForest)
```

Load the data:

```
filename =
"http://archive.ics.uci.edu/ml/machine-learning-databases/housing/housing.d
ata"
housing <- read.table(filename)
colnames(housing) <- c("CRIM", "ZN", "INDUS", "CHAS", "NOX",
                       "RM", "AGE", "DIS", "RAD", "TAX", "PRATIO",
                       "B", "LSTAT", "MDEV")
```

Split it up:

```
housing <- housing[order(housing$MDEV),]
#install.packages("caret")
library(caret)
set.seed(5557)
indices <- createDataPartition(housing$MDEV, p=0.75, list=FALSE)
training <- housing[indices,]
testing <- housing[-indices,]
nrow(training)
nrow(testing)
```

Calculate our model:

```
forestFit <- randomForest(MDEV ~ CRIM + ZN + INDUS + CHAS + NOX
                + RM + AGE + DIS + RAD + TAX + PRATIO
                + B + LSTAT, data=training)
forestFit
Call:
 randomForest(formula = MDEV ~ CRIM + ZN + INDUS + CHAS + NOX +       RM +
AGE + DIS + RAD + TAX + PRATIO + B + LSTAT, data = training)
               Type of random forest: regression
                     Number of trees: 500
No. of variables tried at each split: 4

          Mean of squared residuals: 11.16163
                    % Var explained: 87.28
```

This is one of the more informative displays about a model—we see the model explains 87% of the variable.

Make our prediction:

```
forestPredict <- predict(forestFit, newdata=testing)
See how well the model worked:
diff <- forestPredict - testing$MDEV
sum( (diff - mean(diff) )^2 ) #sum of squares
1391.95553131418
```

This is one of the lowest sum of squares among the models we produced in this chapter.

Summary

In this chapter, we used several machine learning algorithms, some of them in R and Python to compare and contrast. We used naive Bayes to determine how the data might be used. We applied nearest neighbor in a couple of different ways to see our results. We used decision trees to come up with an algorithm for predicting. We tried to use neural network to explain housing prices. Finally, we used the random forest algorithm to do the same—with the best results!

In the next chapter, we will look at optimizing Jupyter notebooks.

10
Optimizing Jupyter Notebooks

Before a Jupyter Notebook is developed you should confront optimizations that should occur before the public starts their access. Optimizations cover a gamut of options running from language-specific issues (use best practice R coding style) to deploying your notebook in a highly available environment.

Deploying notebooks

A Jupyter Notebook is a website. You could host a website on the computer that you are using to display this document. There may be a machine available in your department that is in use as a web server.

If you were to deploy on a local machine you would have a single user website where additional users would be blocked from access or would collide with each other. The first step towards publishing your notebook involves using a hosting service that provides multiple user access.

Deploying to JupyterHub

The predominant Jupyter hosting product currently is JupyterHub. To be clear, JupyterHub is installed into a machine under your control. It provides multi-user access to your notebooks. This means you could install JupyterHub on a machine in your environment and only internal users (multiple internal users) could access it.

When JupyterHub starts it begins a hub or controlling agent. The hub will start an instance of a listener or proxy for Jupyter requests. When the proxy gets requests for Jupyter it turns them over to the hub. If the hub decides this is a new user it will generate a new instance of the Jupyter server and attach all further interactions between that user and Jupyter to their own version of the server. This feature provides multi-user access.

Installing JupyterHub

JupyterHub requires Python 3.3 or better and we will use the Python tool `pip3` to install JupyterHub. The commands to install are:

```
npm install -g configurable-http-proxy
pip3 install jupyterhub
```

Accessing a JupyterHub Installation

We can now start JupyterHub directly from the command line:

```
jupyterhub
```

Instead of the typical `jupyter notebook` that you have been using.

Again, as discussed, JupyterHub is the entry point for users accessing your notebooks. Under the covers it is instantiating Jupyter instances for users.

There are slight differences with the user interface presented as well, as shown in the following screenshot:

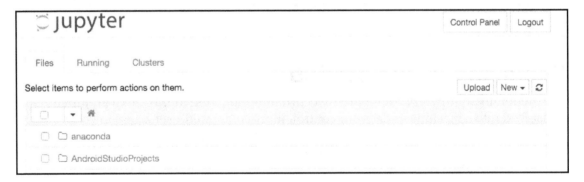

Note the additional buttons on the top right of the screen:

- **Control Panel**: For control of JupyterHub
- **Logout**: **Logout** would be used with the SSL feature of JupyterHub to control access to your notebook

The **Control Panel** gives two options:

- **Stop My Server**: Stops JupyterHub from responding further. Useful if you need to upgrade some part of the system.
- **My Server**: Return to the JupyterHub home page (previous screenshot).

If you start two browser instances on your desktop and access the notebook on JupyterHub you would be presented different information for each user as the user information is separately allocated to each user.

Jupyter hosting

If you want to share your notebook with a larger audience one of the better mechanisms is to use a public hosting service for presenting your notebook. This alleviates the need for some of the extensive security and availability requirements you would incur doing this yourself.

There are an increasing number of (hosting) vendors that are providing Jupyter Notebook hosting as well. A couple of the major vendors are:

- **Rackspace**: Rackspace is particularly geared towards education notebooks where they provide special handling for clients running from the education sector
- **Azure**: The server hosting service by Microsoft—provides full notebook hosting
- **GitHub**: One of the primary source repositories for programming artifacts, such as your notebook

A great feature of these hosting services is you no longer must install any libraries you are accessing from your notebook script. The hosting companies have already downloaded (and maintained and updated) all the libraries that you would normally use. GitHub does this maintenance. The others are pure web-hosting companies and expect you to install any necessary software needed.

Optimizing your script

There are optimizations that you can make to have your notebook scripts run more efficiently. The optimizations are script language dependent. We have covered using Python and R scripts in our notebooks and will cover optimizations that can be made for those two languages.

Jupyter does support additional languages, such as Scala and Spark. The other languages have their own optimization tools and strategies.

Optimizing your Python scripts

Performance tuning your Python scripts can be done using several tools:

- timeit
- Python regular expressions
- String handling
- Loop optimizations
- hotshot profiling

Determining how long a script takes

The timeit function in Python takes a line of code and determines how long it takes to execute. You can also repeatedly execute the same script to see if there are start-up issues that need to be addressed.

timeit is used in this manner:

```
import timeit
t = timeit.Timer("myfunction('Hello World')", "import myfunction")
t.timeit()
3.32132323232
t.repeat(2, 2000000)
[#, #, #]
```

The repeat() function is telling timeit to execute the timed instruction two times at 2,000,000 times each. The numbers displayed after the repeat() call are the three of the times taken as representative of the repeated calls.

You would normally use this to test out a complete function, not something that interacts with the user in any way.

Using Python regular expressions

There are many cases where you need your script to evaluate a string of data, possibly entered by a user. Yes, you could do this by hand, but the Python regular expression processing is extremely efficient and catches all the edge cases that you may not be aware of.

Using Python string handling

Strings are notoriously bad allocations of memory repeatedly as slight changes are made to the string. Furthermore, even small things such as capitalizing a letter in a larger string means a reallocation. Best off to process an entire string, such as capitalizing, in one step as we reduce the reallocation to one shot.

Minimizing loop operations

There are many times when you develop a script that you place steps inside of a loop as it was convenient to do so when developed and probably did not make much difference to performance when running against smaller test data. For example, on any of the scripts in this book I would normally extract a small set of rows to work with. That would provide confidence that I am accessing the data correctly. However, I may have adjusted loop operations to have flagging operations occur. On a smaller dataset of 20 rows or so there is no big effect. However, when I start using the true dataset, which may have millions of rows, the setting of that flag continuously for every row would affect the overall performance of the operation.

However, once you are working with larger data those minor operations that are occurring every time the loop executes become expensive. There are usually operations that can be pulled out of the loop and executed once outside of the loop. For example, if we were looking for the largest number in a loop we would initialize our result outside of the loop to an unrealistic value and inside the loop, if we see the unrealistic value we initialize the result with the first result. This test occurs on every loop operation. Instead we could set the result from the first record BEFORE entering the loop.

Profiling your script

The hotshot profiler is available in Python to give a complete rundown of the execution of your script. Hotshot would have to be installed for you to execute.

It can be used as follows:

```
import hotshot
import myfunction
prof = hotshot.Profile('my_hotshot _stats')
prof.run('myfunction').close()
```

Then to view a summary of the profiler's results use the commands:

```
import hotshot.stats
hotshot.stats.load('my_hotshot_stats').strip_dirs().sort_stats('time').prin
t_stats()
```

Optimizing your R scripts

R also has tools available that will help pinpoint performance issues with your R coding:

- microbenchmark
- Modify a function used frequently
- Optimize name lookup
- Optimize data frame value extraction
- R implementations
- Change algorithm

Using microbenchmark to profile R script

microbenchmark is provided as part of an R library. Once included in your script you then surround the code in question with a microbenchmark tag and once executed the tool will output profiling information for the script in question.

For example, we could have this use:

```
library(microbenchmark)
x <- runif(125)
microbenchmark( mean(x) )
```

Which would exercise the surrounded code 125 times (100 by default) and output profiling information such as:

```
Unit: nanoseconds
    expr  min      lq     mean median      uq    max neval
 sqrt(x)  825   860.5 1212.79  892.5   938.5  12905   100
   x^0.5 3015  3059.5 3776.81 3101.5  3208.0  15215   100
```

Where we are concerned with the mean as a good indication of how long each iteration is taking. We should also notice where there is a large divergence from the mean with very distant min and max values—which is what we have here.

Modifying provided functionality

R allows you to change the behavior of most objects, including most well-known functions provided. An extreme example would be to rework how the mean() function works. Maybe you have insight into the exact nature of the data you are working with and can increase performance accordingly in your special case.

As with the preceding tool, you could exercise the provided functionality and then your implementation, and compare profile information provided by microbenchmark.

Optimizing name lookup

R allows for dynamic naming of objects, so every time you access a variable R must look through a list of scopes to find where the object currently resides.

You may instead use a local cache mechanism to access your exact value directly circumventing R looking for a variable in all scopes.

Optimizing data frame value extraction

With its variety of coding styles R allows you to access a particular value in a data frame in several manners. If your coding is accessing a large data frame frequently to extract singular values it is worthwhile to benchmark different alternatives to see which access method provides the most performance.

Changing R Implementation

R is implemented by a handful of different companies. Each has its own performance spectrum. It may be worthwhile with severe cases to experiment with different R implementations to determine which works best for you. It may be difficult to change the R engine used by Jupyter.

Changing algorithms

Whenever you program your notebook you have taken an approach to solving the problem. The approach is referred to as the *algorithm* used. Your algorithm may include looping over records or querying records inside of the database directly to obtain the records of interest. Many times, you will select an algorithm early in the process which appears to work adequately. There may be other algorithms which solve the problem in a much more efficient manner.

The largest boost to any programming implementation will come by changing the overall approach to handling. Unfortunately, this is the hardest change to accomplish as redesign and rewrite of your coding is required. And even then, like the other techniques, you need to compare benchmarks of your different approaches to make sure the new approach is better.

Monitoring Jupyter

As with the earlier discussions in this chapter on optimization, you can also use programming tools to monitor the overall interactions of your notebook. The predominant tool for Linux/Mac environments is `memory_profiler`. If you start this tool then your notebook, the profiler will keep track of memory use of your notebook.

With this record of information points you may be able to adjust your programmatic memory allocation to be smaller in profile if you find a large memory use occurring. For example, the profiler may highlight that you are creating (and dropping) a large memory item continuously inside of a loop. When you go back to your coding you realize this memory access could be pulled out of the loop and just done once or that size of the allocation could be minimized easily.

Caching your notebook

Caching is a common programming practice to speed up performance. If the computer does not have to reload a section of code or variable or file, but can just access directly from a cache this will improve performance.

There is a mechanism to cache your notebook if you are deploying into a Docker space. Docker is a mechanism for virtualizing code over many instances in one machine. It has become common practice to do so in the Java programming world. Luckily, Docker is very flexible and a method has been determined to use Jupyter in Docker as well. Once in Docker, it is a minor adjustment to automatically cache your pages in Docker. The underlying tool used is `memcached`, yet another widespread common tool for caching anything, in this case Jupyter Notebooks.

Securing a notebook

Securing a notebook can be accomplished by several methods such as:

- Manage authorization
- Securing notebook content

Managing notebook authorization

A notebook can be secured to use username/password authorization. Authorization is on by default in your notebook. Under Jupyter it is token/password instead of username/password as a token is more open to interpretation. See Jupyter documentation on implementing authorization as this has changed slightly over time.

Securing notebook content

A notebook has possible security issues with several parts of standard content that are secured automatically by Jupyter:

- Untrusted HTML is sanitized
- Untrusted JavaScript is not executed
- HTML and JavaScript in markdown cells is not trusted
- Notebook output is not trusted
- Other HTML or JavaScript in the notebook is not trusted

Where trust comes down to the question: Did the user do this or did the Jupyter script? Untrusted means it will not be generated.

Sanitized code is wrapped to force the values to be text display only—no executed code will be generated. For example, if your notebook cell were to produce HTML, such as an additional H1 header tag, Jupyter would sanitize the output such that the raw HTML, in this case something like <H1>Additional Heading</H1> would produce the raw HTML with the H1 tags rather than the desired effect of an HTML heading appearing on your page.

Scaling Jupyter Notebooks

Scaling is the process of providing very large numbers of concurrent users to a notebook without a degradation in performance. The one vendor that is doing this today is Azure. They have thousands of pages and users working at scale daily.

Most amazingly this is a **free** service.

Sharing Jupyter Notebooks

Jupyter Notebooks can be shared by placing the notebook on a server (there are several kinds) or converting the notebook to another format (it will not be interactive, but the content will be available).

Sharing Jupyter Notebook on a notebook server

Built into the notebook configuration are extensions that can be used to expose a notebook server, directly. The notebook configuration can be generated using the following command:

```
Jupyter Notebook –generate-config
```

In the resulting jupyter_notebook_config.py file there are settings that can be used to set:

- IP/port address of your notebook
- Encryption certificate location
- Password

By setting this and starting Jupyter you should be able to access the notebook at the IP address specified from other machines in your network.

 You should work with your network security personnel before doing so.

Sharing encrypted Jupyter Notebook on a notebook server

If you specify the certificate information correctly in the previous configuration file the notebook will only be accessible over HTTPS or a secure, encrypted channel.

Sharing notebook on a web server

Another part of the configuration file is the `tornado_settings`. This set of settings describes the web server that will channel web traffic to your notebook. Again, once these settings are in place you can access your notebook through the web server-using the web servers IP address.

This might be useful to present notebook access as part of your existing website.

Sharing notebook on Docker

Docker is a framework that provides for hosting instances of software based on a small configuration file, the `Dockerfile`. Docker allows for multiple instances of software to be instantiated automatically as needed. So, we would have multiple instances of our notebook available to users. Users would not be able to distinguish the multiple instances as they just reference the one notebook. Docker redirects user traffic to one or the other instances based on initial connection to the system.

The `Dockerfile` has the environment settings that tell the Docker system what system components need to be present in an instance in order for the referenced object, in this case a notebook, can be executed.

Converting a notebook

You can also share a notebook with others by converting the notebook to a readable form for recipients. Notebooks can be converted to a number of formats using the **Download As** feature in the notebook **File** menu.

Notebooks can be converted in this way to the formats:

- **<language> format**: This option is dependent on the language used to create the notebook. For example, an R notebook would have the choice to **Download as R script.**
- **HTML**: This representation is the HTML encoding to display the page as it appears in your notebook using HTML constructs.
- **Markdown**: Markdown is a simple display tag format used by some older Linux systems.
- **reST**: Another markdown type of format that has simpler display constructs than HTML.
- **PDF.**

Versioning a notebook

A common practice in the programming world is to maintain a history of the changes made to a program. Over time the different versions of the program are maintained in a software repository where the programmer can retrieve prior versions to return to an older, working state of their program.

In the previous section we mentioned placing your notebook on GitHub. Git is a software repository in wide use. GitHub is an internet-based instance of Git. Once you have any software in Git it will automatically be versioned. The next time you update your notebook in GitHub. Git will take the current instance, store it as a version in your history, and place the new instance as the current—where anyone accessing your GitHub repository will see the latest version by default.

Summary

In this chapter, we deployed our notebook to a set of different environments. We looked into optimizations that can be made to our notebook scripts. We learned about different ways to share our notebook. Lastly, we looked into converting our notebook for users without access to Jupyter.

Index

3

3D data
  plotting 86, 87

A

Advanced Micro Devices (AMD) 41
airplane arrival time
  predicting 126, 128, 129
arbitrary search of ratings 183, 184
average ratings
  visualizing, by cuisine 182, 183

C

caching 217
cell 7
code markdown
  used, for publishing notebook 161
columns
  adding, to data frame 143
  manipulating, in data frame 51
concepts, Jupyter
  cell 7
  kernel 7
  notebook 7
CSV file
  reading 131, 132, 133, 134, 135, 136, 138
CSV
  JSON, converting to 171, 172
current cell 7

D

data frame
  column, adding to 143
  columns, manipulating in 51
  converting, to dplyr table 139
  filtering 63

groupby function, using in 50, 51
  outliers, calculating in 52
  rows, filtering in 142
  sorting 64, 65
  summary, obtaining on calculated field 144
data scraping
  with Python notebook 41, 42, 43, 44
data value ranges
  overview 139
data
  analyzing, Spark used 90
  cleaning, with tidyr package 147, 149, 151
  manipulating, with dplyr package 138
  piping, between functions 144
datasets
  combining 97, 98, 99, 100, 101
  sampling 140
decision trees
  about 198
  in Python 201
  in R 199, 200, 201
  reference 198
Docker
  installing, on machine 36
  notebook, sharing on 219
  reference 35
  using, with Jupyter 34
dplyr package
  used, for manipulating data 138
dplyr table
  data frame, converting to 139

E

encrypted Jupyter Notebook
  sharing, on notebook server 219
Excel files
  reading, pandas used 49

F

FFT (Fourier Transforms) 58
filter function
  used, for filtering rows in data frame 142
font markdown
  used, for publishing notebook 159
functions
  data, piping between 144

G

GitHub
  notebook, sharing on 37
glyph 153
glyph ready data
  visualizing 153, 154, 155, 156, 157, 158, 159
Google Drive
  notebook, sharing on 37
groupby function
  using, in data frame 50, 51
grouped data
  summary, obtaining on 146

H

heading markdown
  used, for publishing notebook 160
heavy-duty processing functions
  using, in Jupyter 45
histogram
  drawing, of social data 83, 84, 86
human density map
  creating 80

I

interactive visualization 77, 78

J

JSON
  about 171
  converting, to CSV 171, 172
  loading, into Spark 101, 102
Jupyter hosting 211
Jupyter Notebooks
  scaling 218
  security 38

sharing 218
sharing, on notebook server 218
sharing, ways 36, 37
Jupyter project display
  Cell menu 16, 17
  Edit menu 14, 15
  File menu 13, 14
  Help menu 18
  Icon toolbar 18
  Insert menu 16
  Kernel menu 17, 18
  View menu 15, 16
  viewing 12
Jupyter tabs
  Clusters tab 9
  Files tab 9
  Running tab 9
Jupyter user interface 8
Jupyter
  about 7
  actions, performing 9, 10
  concepts 7
  Docker, using with 34
  heavy-duty data processing functions, using 45
  industry data science usage 20
  installing, on web server 37
  monitoring 216
  NumPy functions, using in 45, 46
  object manipulation 11
  panda data frames 61, 62
  pandas, used for reading Excel files 49
  pandas, used for reading text files 48
  pandas, using in 48
  R, setting up for 107
  real life examples 21
  SciPy Fourier Transforms, using in 58
  SciPy integration, using in 53
  SciPy interpolation, using in 57
  SciPy linear algebra, using in 59
  SciPy optimization, using in 55, 56
  SciPy, using in 53
JupyterHub installation
  accessing 210, 211
JupyterHub
  installing 210

notebooks, deploying to 209

K
kernel 7

L
list markdown
  used, for publishing notebook 160

M
MapReduce
  example 92, 93
markdown
  notations 162
  used, for publishing notebook 159
MIME (Multi-purpose Internet Mail Extension)
    format 36
mutate function
  column, adding to data frame 143

N
Naive Bayes
  about 189
  with Python 192
  with R 189, 190, 191, 192
nb2mail
  reference 36
nbviewer
  reference 37
nearest neighbor estimator 193
nearest neighbor
  with Python 195
  with R 193, 194
neural networks
  about 203
  in R 203, 204
notebook authorization
  managing 217
notebook content
  securing 217
notebook server
  encrypted Jupyter Notebook, sharing on 219
  Jupyter Notebooks, sharing on 218
notebook, publishing

code markdown used 161
font markdown used 159
heading markdown used 160
list markdown used 160
markdown used 159
table markdown used 161
notebook
  about 7
  caching 217
  converting 220
  deploying 209
  deploying, to JupyterHub 209
  securing 217
  sharing, on Docker 219
  sharing, on GitHub 37
  sharing, on Google Drive 37
  sharing, on web server 219
  versioning 220
NumPy functions
  using, in Jupyter 45, 46

O
outliers
  calculating, in data frame 52

P
panda data frames 61, 62
pandas
  used, for reading Excel files 49
  used, for reading text files 48
  used, for working with data frames 50
  using, in Jupyter 48
pivot() function 103
Plotly
  about 79
  using, for plotting 79
prediction
  making, R used 72, 73, 74, 76
  making, scikit-learn used 67, 68, 69, 71
public Docker service
  using 35
Python implementation
  of Naive Bayes 192
  of nearest neighbor 196
Python scripts

optimizing 212, 213, 214
Python
  used, for comparing ratings 180, 182

Q

quantile() function
  99% quantile, obtaining 145

R

R data analysis
  of 2016 US election demographics 108, 109,
    110
  of 2016 voter registration 111, 112, 113, 114,
    116, 117, 118, 119
  of 2016 voting 111, 112, 113, 114, 116, 117,
    118, 119
  of changes in college admissions 120, 121, 123,
    124
R implementation
  of Naive Bayes 189, 190, 191, 192
  of nearest neighbor 193, 194
R scripts
  optimizing 214, 215, 216
R
  setting up, for Jupyter 107
  used, for making prediction 72, 73, 74, 76
random forests
  about 205
  in R 206, 207
ratings
  comparing, Python used 180, 182
real-life examples, Jupyter
  Consumer products, R - marketing effectiveness
    31, 33
  Finance, Python - European call option valuation
    21, 22
  Finance, Python - Monte Carlo pricing 23
  Gambling, R - betting analysis 25
  Insurance, R - non-life insurance pricing 27, 29
relationships
  determining, between number of ratings and
    ratings 184, 187, 188
rows
  filtering, in data frame 142

S

scikit-learn
  used, for making prediction 67, 68, 69, 71
SciPy Fourier Transforms
  using, in Jupyter 58
SciPy integration
  using, in Jupyter 53
SciPy interpolation
  using, in Jupyter 57
SciPy linear algebra
  using, in Jupyter 59
SciPy optimization
  using, in Jupyter 55, 56
SciPy
  using, in Jupyter 53
scripts
  executing 19, 20
  optimizing 212
security, Jupyter Notebooks
  access control 38
  malicious content 38
shiny dashboard
  creating 162
  publishing 167
  R application coding 163, 164
Spark pivot
  using 103
Spark
  guidelines, for Windows installation 90
  JSON, loading into 101, 102
  used, for analyzing data 90
SparkSession
  using 94, 95, 96
SQL
  using 94, 95, 96
standalone dashboards
  building 168, 169
summarize function 144
summary
  obtaining, on grouped data 146

T

table markdown
  used, for publishing markdown 161

text files
  reading, pandas used 48
tidyr package
  used, for cleaning data 147, 149, 151
TSV (tab-separated value) 108

W

web server
  Jupyter, installing on 37
  notebook, sharing on 219

Y

Yelp reviews evaluation
  about 172
  correlation, determining between ratings and
    number of reviews 178
  model of reviews, building 179, 180
  most rated firms, finding 176
  ratings, finding for top-rated firm 176
  review spread 174, 175
  summary data 173, 174
  top rated firms, finding 175